Auto da fé

*… Licenziando queste cronache
ho l'impressione di buttarle nel fuoco
e di liberarmene per sempre (E. Montale)*

Susanna Berti Franceschi
Gian Ugo Berti

The Archetypes Of Fear

Stories of Love, Memory and Loss

Authors' Biographies

Susanna Berti Franceschi is Vice-President of the Angiolo and Maria Teresa Berti National Historical Society. As part of her role, she is also the Director of the scientific committee for historical research and is in charge of organising conferences on behalf of the Society. In 2011, she chaired the following two conferences: «Anarchist Attempts to Assassinate Mussolini», which inluded a paper on the role of Violet Gibson; and «Carlo Pisacane: Action and the Revolutionary Idea», with a paper on the figure of Enrichetta Di Lorenzo. Her main area of interest is Gender History and the role of women in culture and power, with a particular focus on the Middle Ages.

Her previous works include: *On Queens, Saints and Witches* (*Di regine di sante e di streghe*) for Elmi's Words; *The Woodpecker* (*Il picchio*) for Rupe Mutevoli; *Ashes* (*Ceneri*) for Aletti.

Gian Ugo Berti, neurosurgeon, born in 1947, four times UNAMSI National Scientific Career Award (the National Scientific Medical Information Union) in 2009 and SOI (Italian Ophthalmologic Society) Award in 2010, collaborated with the Editorial group "La Repubblica-Espresso" since 1978. Is president of the "Angiolo and Maria Teresa Berti" Foundation, an institution of historical and cultural character.

Gian Ugo Berti has been the director responsible for "Radio Livorno Città Aperta" for ten years, an ISIS (Institute for Health Care) employee. For several years wrote for the IPD (Institute for Parliamentarians Defense) periodical, for the Italian Ministry of Health, for the Higher Italian Institute of Health and supported the re-elaboration of the Disability Act.

Susanna Berti Franceschi
Gian Ugo Berti

The Archetypes Of Fear

Stories of Love, Memory and Loss

Author's Foreword

Of all the psychological behaviours and of all the emotions that govern our relationship with external reality, fear is, perhaps, and the most adaptive and "corrective".

It is through fear that we learn to recognise danger and it is on the basis of this learning – a path which is itself not without risk (I might mention the child who, burning himself, acquires a fear of fire) – we develop strategies of prevention in order to avoid danger.

It is due to fear that evolution has favoured humans over other species.

As humans, we relate the emotion of fear first to memory, and then to our own hypothesis of danger. It is in this way that we are able, both as individuals and as a species, to evaluate the risk of a given event.

The most ancient fears can be traced back to the first bipedal hominids. These fears have entered the collective memory and are common to all human beings. They are fears which are acquired at birth and which do not require direct experience.

Let us take a simple example: earthquakes.

All of us, despite having no direct experience of this event, are instinctively afraid of earthquakes. Carl

Gustav Jung, the great psychoanalyst and scholar of Transcendentalism and the paranormal, defined these sorts of fear as archetypes.

There are also individual fears, those that are born and develop on the basis of a traumatic experience or painful event. If you are bitten by a dog, you will necessarily be afraid of any dog which tries to approach you.

It is necessary at this point to distinguish fear from phobias. Fear stems from a real event which has caused pain or danger. Phobias (the full distinction is too lengthy to explain here) are also born of imagined events. Simply put, fear is a part of reality, while phobias belong to the realm of the symbolic.

In this brief dissertation on fear we might say, therefore, that there exist both fears as old as man, as well as collective fears relating to more recent events in human history.

One such example, which is today both extremely widespread and a source of collective anxiety, is the fear of the end of the world and of the effect on humanity of nuclear and natural disasters.

Some might argue that as early as the year 1000, humanity was afflicted by a collective madness heralding catastrophic events which, it was assumed, would bring about the end of the known world. I, in fact, consider such prophecies as a precursor of the fear which we experience today. It should also be said that a fear of the world ending with the first millennium originated in what many saw as God's inevitable punishment of man for his sins and transgressions.

In the wake of this fear there flourished a number of religious movements and mystics, all claiming to be able to redirect the benevolent eye of the Eternal Father back towards to humanity. The fear of the third millennium is more invasive and destructive: it is no longer God who punishes and destroys, but man, through the misuse of science, who will bring about the final catastrophe.

Such a fear is characterised by depression and a sense of inevitability, in which man is the conscious, but equally helpless spectator of his own destruction. These short stories speak precisely of this: the terrifying hypotheses which one famous film defined as "The Day After Tomorrow", the next day, or centuries or millennia later.

But, as the title implies, they also speak of more than just the human condition, something which has and will always remain unchanged throughout man's collective journey: they tell of love, of memory, of nostalgia, of marginalisation and the sense of being different. For I believe that to truly understand man, one must also know his fears.

SUSANNA BERTI FRANCESCHI

Thoughts:
Chochise and H.P. Lovecraft

The Creation Of Heaven

The First Lady arranged the stars
To help the Moon to shine.
One by one, she set them in order,
In the form of shimmering in animals
hung in the night sky.
But the Old Coyote broke free in his joy,
And scattered the stars as you see them today.

(Cochise, *Songs of the American Indians*, Algonquian Blackfoot)

The most merciful thing in the world, I think, is the inability of the human mind to correlate all its contents. We live on a placid island of ignorance in the midst of black seas of infinity, and it was not meant that we should voyage far. The sciences, each straining in its own direction, have hitherto harmed us little; but some day the piecing together of dissociated knowledge will open up such terrifying vistas of reality, and of our frightful position therein, that we shall either go mad from the revelation or flee from the deadly light into the peace and safety of a new dark age.

(H.P. Lovecraft, *The Call of Cthulhu*)

Spiders

The little spider moved quickly, barely brushing the tip of her shoe.

She drew back instinctively, her heart pounding in her chest.

«Don't be silly, there's nothing to worry about, it's not time, their moment has not yet come».

She turned her head to see if the windows and the door were closed and if the wooden boards she had put up to support the old fixtures still held.

She saw no holes. The tables were fixed in place where she had nailed them down, as she had done every morning for months.

She moved with experience in the darkened room: she knew every edge, every corner. In the map of her mind she saw every chair and every piece of furniture. The shelf on which the book lay was in the opposite corner to the stove.

There it was safe from the heat and flames which warmed her food.

The book was all that was left, as precious as the tin of beans and canned meat, or the few remaining biscuits.

She was the book, her voice, her thought and memory, now faded and lost.

She took the book and sat down on the mattress to read as she always did.

The pages appeared more fragile than usual, the paper creased, as if ready to crumble at anything but the lightest touch.

She opened the book to page 236. She did not like that page; its words did not match her knowledge.

What the page described did not adhere to any image so far registered by her mind: a lake. Page 236 did not describe what a lake was supposed to be, but it did speak of the sky. She knew what the sky was, even if it was a different sky to the one she could see.

It did not matter, she had a task to fulfil: to read and memorise the text, and perhaps, one day, to pass on this memory to someone else.

If there would ever be someone else.

The spider had moved to just below the table and stood motionless, without showing the slightest intention of climbing up to confront the clean plate which she had left there.

It was not time yet, it was too soon, the hour had not yet come. Even so, you could never know if spiders were capable, purely on a whim, of disrupting the precise and long-established sequence of events.

She immersed herself in her reading, forcing herself, as usual, to turn the words into images: buzzard, what could it be? It was something that moved, or rather, flew. Maybe it was living animal, like spiders; but it was definitely not a spider.

Spiders she knew well, all of them: their colours, species, habits, the most ferocious, the harmless ones, the males, and the females, which could deposit millions of eggs in a crevice in the wall. After that it was certain death. Buzzards, no, she had no idea what colour they were.

Many years ago, her father had kept, in a small wooden box, six or seven sticks, each with a beautiful tip.

Sometimes, only very rarely, he took a sheet of paper, already used, sometimes hundreds of times, and invited her to slide the sticks over its surface and try to imagine things, to bring them to life on the page.

The sticks left a trace and her father, with the memory of his own father, guided her hand so that sometimes, marks appeared on the paper which could lend a face to the words of the book.

But her father had died too soon to pass the memory on to her, or perhaps she had been young to learn it for herself.

Her mother had no memory and did not love her; she considered it unnecessary.

She was engaged in a methodical war against the spiders and succeeding in killing many. Deep down, she knew she had been right.

If they had survived it was not because of her father's memory, but thanks to the constant battles of her mother against the spiders.

Reading kept her occupied. She read the pages over and over again, systematically and with determination.

Every single word had to penetrate her mind; understanding and pleasure did not matter. It was an ancient and necessary rite; this was what memory had taught her.

The paper was so fragile now that it threatened to crumble in her hands; but she had learned a lightness of touch which did not damage the book.

Never once had she asked herself what would happen when the book was no longer there. The book was all that remained of times past and without it she had no memory, and without memory she had no reason to live.

The third time she read the page she knew it was time to go out. The book never failed to regulate time.

She closed it gently and put it back on the shelf, wrapped in its white cloth.

She put on her hood and over the hood, her cloak, to protect her shoulders. She slipped on her gloves and, finally, her white waxed overshoes.

Her father had told her that the overshoes were as ancient as the book and that they had once belonged to the men who came through the fire, without which they would not have made it across.

She leaned the ladder against the wall in order to reach the skylight to the shelter: it was time. She could stay outside for forty-five minutes before the heat burned the inside of her body and her organs melted.

She needed water and she took the metre to measure how warm it was. These were old customs, each of which served a purpose. Or perhaps they did not.

She went over to the ladder. The little spider was still crouched at the foot of the table. Casually, she crushed it with the tip of her shoe, pressing down again on what was left of it with her heel.

She placed one foot on the first rung and began to climb. Outside, the immense collapsed sun gradually began to illuminate the earth, growing ever wider in the profound darkness.

A Warm Sun

The warm sun was just rising on the horizon, there were the tops of the mountains bowed like a cradle of rock. He prepared to take over the watch.
The new morning gave him little to feel happy about and he thought of how he would rather have remained a little longer in the warmth of his thermal cell.

But the work had to be finished on time, and time was almost up.

Soon, all of the equipment would have to be dismantled and the whole group would be transferred elsewhere to continue with their observation. They would carry on until they were able to decide.

To decide what he did not know, for no one had ever told him and he did not dream of asking.

He was just a technician, a good worker, a professional with years of experience, much appreciated by his superiors, but nothing more.

It was others who had the knowledge and who made the decisions.

He settled himself as comfortably as possible on the wet grass and pulled out the "tools" of his trade.

Before long they would emerge from their burrows and he had to be ready and alert.

But after so many years, his eyes already knew what to look out for, even if his attention was likely to drift.

The rays of the rising sun shone on the frost, illuminating it with the magic of a thousand sparkling colours.

Like a child, he sat transfixed by the phenomenon of the reflected light.

He knew from the refraction of light that it would all take place within am instant.

And sure enough, it soon started, following the same pace as ever.

The burrows all sprung open more or less simultaneously and the creatures began to emerge.

The sequence was the same as always: some were isolated, some in pairs, others in small groups.

All moved in predetermined directions.

One led them to a small clearing in which the creatures piled up against each other to await the big log; or at least, this was the nickname he had given it, for it seemed just like a large, stocky log.

When the log slid towards the clearing the creatures seemed to awake from their slumber and begin to shake.

Given their state of agitation, he assumed that the log was very important to them.

Perhaps it was some sort of tribal totem.

Perhaps the creatures were evolved enough to have a totem. This was not, however, a question for him to answer.

The log slid away with painful slowness. He was always amazed at the calmness with which the creatures moved.

It was possible to follow their movements for some time.

Some, however, remained in their burrows, choosing to emerge later, or not to show themselves at all for a whole rotation of the sun, or even longer.

Those which came forth in the second wave seemed less agitated than the first and moved with an even greater sense of calm.

They dragged along what he assumed to be the young of the species, tiny but highly active and unpredictable creatures, like small spiders, which they treated with the utmost care.

At times they seemed to control the larger ones, even if he believed this to be impossible, contradicting as it did every rule known to him.

The sun began to dry the earth, leaving behind little pools of water.

He dipped his finger in a nearby pool and sucked the cool liquid with pleasure.

His whole body shuddered with delight and he was immediately left with a feeling of guilt.

The creatures drank large quantities without any problem, their bodies most likely being composed in large part of water.

They drank often, but expelled the water just as quickly.

He leant his head on the grass and gazed up at the brilliant blue sky. The sun shone into eyes, but he had no need to close them.

His heart became heavy as the weight of his memories took his breath away, so that for a moment, he almost forgot his work and the creatures.

It was time for him to go home.

Too many years he had wandered, studying creatures across many different galaxies.

Together with the scientists, their expedition had led them in search of a planet which might be compatible with their needs, compatible with the needs of his species.

The images of his barren and dying land appeared before his great lidless eyes.

The endless stretches of desert, where every drop of water was a precious commodity and where, for hundreds of years, there had not grown so much as a single blade of grass.

He thought of his precious love and the last time that had seen her, a small, helpless thing, her rough skin, as was traditional for wives, covered in yellow earth.

The water reserve attached to her thermal suit, she had watched him leave.

How many years had passed since then?

How many thousands of light years now stretched out between them?

There had never been another creature, even if he had seen many, who had seemed more beautiful to him than she did.

He saw her now, standing bravely against their great black dying sun.

Although the stones weighed heavy on his heart and his memories cut him like tiny blades, now, as he did every day, he turned to makes notes for their mission.

«Day 146 of observation.

Planet 568 of the yjw galaxy.

The creatures which inhabit it call it Earth…».

The Wait

Non fu l'orgoglio a perderci,
fu il desiderio di essere umani.

JOHN MILTON

The shaft of light pierced her eyes as it shone through the crack in the dome.

Before long, the pale sun would have cancelled out, one by one, each of the six moons.

It was not yet time to go out, for she knew that the blind giants were hungry and might still be on the prowl, silently in search of prey.

She would have to wait a little longer, at least until the first grey light rose over the heat. She was used to waiting; time had no real meaning for her.

She remained seated on the turret, which served her as a stool, her long legs crossed beneath her like a heron.

She had once seen a photo of a heron in an old book (made of paper!) left behind by an expedition party from Earth, and she had seen something of herself in its noble composure. But that had been a long time ago, some three or four hundred years before.

Time to her simply meant waiting.

She passed her hand over her head in order to feel something, anything. Her shorn silver hair scratched the palm of her hand and she immediately felt the comfort of a warmth she had not yet forgotten.

A plaintive moan like the mewling of a kitten suddenly woke her from her reverie.

«Coming Hal, I'll be right there».

She walked with quick light steps towards a small room on the far side of the dome and moved in the darkness towards the voice.

«Did you wake up?».

At first there was just a squeak then, the small and laboured voice of a man emerged from the damaged lungs.

«Did you see anything? Flashes in the sky?».

«It's still early».

«No it isn't! There are only three light years between us and them, a mere flash in space».

«It's still early I tell you. They'll be here».

She gently lifted the man's head a little, all the while trying not to cause him any pain.

«I'll get you something to drink. Do you need something to drink? Some Basor?».

The man did not reply. He seemed lost in some dream of his own, his eyes fixed on images she could not see».

She took the bag of Basor anyway and slipped the thin tube into Hal's mouth.

There were ten bags left, only ten. If she only drank as much as she needed to stay moving, they had exactly fifteen days left.

Hal seemed drowsy. His skin was translucent, almost transparent, so that small pale pink vessels traced a sort of arabesque across his face.

Hal had once been so handsome, a perfect specimen of their race, with broad shoulders, long muscular legs, sculpted features, and a brilliant smile which cheered even the darkest moments.

How long had it been? A long time? A short while? Did time exist? Could it be measured? Did time even matter down there? And emotions, did they matter? To feel, to sense pain, joy, fear, regret; they were changing emotions, but at the same time, sure and stable in their existence.

There had been feelings of love between them, warm currents of scents, sounds and perceptions which crossed the void around them.

They were emotions long gone, before the waiting and sense of fear had first taken over.

The fourth moon, the giant red moon, was just beginning to fade. It was the project which had brought them there.

The project had involved hundreds of scientists from all over Earth's Federation.

The greatest minds had come together, after centuries of disagreement over their varying abilities and priorities, to decide the project for the relocation of Earth.

She had not been part of the first phase of the project. In fact, she could not remember having existed before their arrival on that planet.

This had always bothered her, not existing "before", not having memories of her home planet.

Out of nowhere she felt a searing cramp in her left hand, a piercing shock which ran through her whole body, before exploding like lightening in her brain.

She needed the Basor, for without it the shocks would have continued to come in quick succession, eventually immobilising her so that she would be unable to reach Hal if he called.

She took a bag and barely squeezing the tube, let a few big drops of the liquid fall between her lips.

It ought to be enough.

She returned to watching through the crack in the dome and called up her memories again like a moving picture. The film may have been out of focus, but her emotions were as real as they had been back then.

She had believed in the project, she had loved it, and she had been prepared to do anything to carry it forward. She felt as if she had been one with the project, as if she had been born for it, to make it succeed at all costs, and Hal with her, more than her even. They had worked tirelessly to process the data.

The data could mean the difference between life and death.

The last moon disappeared moments before the sun came into view.

A sun that did not give off warmth, but barely illuminated the endless expanse of rock.

She saw the shadows of the giants moving quickly to hide themselves in the rocky crevices.

They were cruel creatures, the giants, which preyed on and devoured anything that moved.

Blind and deaf, they relied on antennae above their bulging, unseeing eyes in order to sense creatures and things.

They would vanish in the first weak light of dawn, which is when the teams would emerge to carry out their work and their research.

There were no more teams. That had all been a long time, many emotions ago.

There was no more laughter, no more ribald jokes, stories, memories, legends, there was nothing left: only her, Hal and ten bags of Basor.

She could no longer hear the gasping of Hal and the silence had become like a fog which enveloped her thoughts.

She stood still for a moment, those long legs which had leapt with ease over rocks as tall as a man now inert, no longer responsive to the feeble commands of her mind.

The quake took her by surprise, as thousands of small shapes, bright and round, danced for a moment before her eyes. In that moment a rush of warmth entered and left her head before she had time to stop it, to understand.

The sun now hung high in the sky.

The reconnaissance ship landed with the sun still in the same position.

Four figures entered the dome, their silvery blue suits denoting their rank of earthmen.

The shortest was the last to enter.

«Mission 12 data acquisition survivors?».

«No survivors Commander. No bodies».

«Two androids detected, both short-circuited. First project model».

Fever

«The oldest and strongest emotion of mankind is fear, and the oldest and strongest kind of fear is fear of the unknown».

(H.P. Lovecraft, *Supernatural Horror in Literature*)

Sometimes she thought that there had never been a past and that there would never be a future, at least for her.

Nothing could return to the way it was before and all that had not been achieved weighed like a stone on her heart.

That evening in mid-autumn, an autumn with no leaves, she walked the usual roads, the safe ones that she knew well, from which she could anticipate any unexpected dangers. If it was indeed possible to anticipate unexpected dangers, for she did not believe that it was.

She had not been like this before, in her life. She had foreseen nothing, and that which she had foreseen she had not known how to avoid.

To be able to see an event beforehand had allowed her to travel with greater determination.

No more. Now she only needed the determination to survive. She was drawn to a good-sized dustbin, apparently not yet known to the feral dogs.

She approached it beating a steady rhythm on the pavement with her the iron tip of her stick. It would be enough to scare off any rats or dogs, for the time being at least.

The rats were worse than the dogs: as large as moles, with long pointed teeth, razor sharp. They attacked regardless of whether they were hungry or not and their bite was often fatal.

They carried the fever, but it did not harm them.

No rat had ever died of the fever.

In fact, as far as she knew, no animal had ever died of the fever.

Men, yes, many, perhaps all of them. It was months since she had seen another human being.

But the bin was there and possibly contained something to eat. Even if it was rubbish, what was good enough for the rats was good enough for her.

She lifted the dirty lid of the rusty bin. The stench of rot which came out of it seized her throat like a vice as the taste of bile rose from her stomach.

This was not the time to be squeamish, for there could be something edible inside. All she had to do was find it in the midst of all that rot and pull it out without being bitten by any unwanted guests.

She began to rummage inside with her stick: there were greasy sheets of paper, perforated shreds of plastic, empty containers of all types, pieces of bread and biscuits entirely covered in green mould. Suddenly, a piece of rubbish made her jump backwards as a rat leapt from the bin, scurrying away, more frightened by the stick than by her.

If there was a rat then there must be something edible, or why else would it waste its precious time rummaging around in there.

And there it was, a half-opened packet of sliced bread. Not bad, she thought. It was nearly whole and, reassuringly, the colour was fairly fresh.

«Is this what you were after, my little friend?».

She reached inside, too hungry to be afraid.

She pulled out the packet of bread and held it up to admire it: the pretty cellophane wrapping still bore the red and blue mark of the brand and incredibly, on the underside, the logo of the supermarket.

She slipped the packet inside her jacket and held it close like a child.

«Let's go home. We can spend the evening together!».

She wasn't so stupid as to start eating it in the middle of the road. To do so would have been too great a temptation for some lovely animal that was just as hungry as she was.

She set off towards home, even though her shelter could not exactly be called as such.

The desolate streets stretched out before her, great tracks of cement made even larger by the total absence of people. The huge buildings and imposing skyscrapers which lined the road on either side seemed like grim sentinels of death.

It was the silence that frightened her more than that desert of cement though.

It was an ominous, invasive silence, broken only by an occasional squeak or growl, and that roaring wind which rushed through the open and broken doors of the skyscrapers.

She walked with her head down, as if seeing only confirmed once more that this was now her life, depriving her of the subconscious hope that it would continue. How to live and, above all, why, were not questions she wished to ask herself. It is true though that when everything is lost, you no longer ask yourself anything and life seems to carry on as if driven by inertia, like a ball which has come back to earth and continues to roll for a little on its own.

She turned into the fourth street, and then the fifth, quickening her pace because the small resort which she called home, there in the park, was now close by. The four wooden planks which she used to block and protect the entrance were still there, just as she had left them, and the thin yellow ribbons tied to them fluttered in the breeze. Good, no animal, or no big animal at least, had got in.

Moving a plank aside, she opened up a gap wide enough to pass and immediately put it back in its place. As insecure and unsafe it was she could finally relax, for she was home.

She took off her jacket and sat down on the mattress which served as bed, desk and table.

Carefully, she opened the packet and began to eat a slice of the soft white bread.

Tearing it into tiny pieces, she held each piece in her mouth for as long as possible. She had long ago learned that greed did not satisfy hunger.

She finished the slice and hid the rest beneath the mattress.

She did not know when she would next find food.

The light outside was gradually fading. Soon it would be dark and the great rats, friends of the night, would begin to roam the streets, terrorising her as they did every night so that her sleep was restless and interrupted.

She touched her forehead and the skin of her neck. They were dry, no sweat, no swellings.

The fever had not entered her body.

She could not remember how it had started or where, but she did remember how the fever had overcome her family, and the memory of it still gripped her with a sensation that was somewhere between discomfort and disbelief.

Bedford-Stuyvesant (New York City, 2053)

30

In the kitchen, the usual, reassuring chaos of the holidays reigned, as the house was filled with people, all waiting, as her father would say, for the trumpet call to lunch.

The large table was completely covered in Maddy's drawings, in the midst of which stood out a huge and brightly coloured puffer fish, somewhat proud, with an unlikely pair of angel's wings.

Maddy had had a fixation with wings ever since the pastor had told the children that wings served us to fly faster into the arms of the Lord.

As she was a generous little girl, from that day forth she had given all the characters in her drawings great pairs of white feathered wings.

Rupert was stretched out on the ground, lost in an imaginary battle between toy cars and small robots. Mum floated around between the two work surfaces in the kitchen (she had been a classical ballet dancer and when she moved, even if it was only to cook the Christmas turkey, she seemed to float ethereally on the tips of her toes). On one she was preparing breaded cutlets, according to the Italian tradition, and on the other she was covering the chicken in flour to put with the curry and rice, according to the English tradition.

Dad had had a great-great-grandfather from the Veneto, while Mum had come from London to study dance in New York and never left. Out of fairness, our Sunday lunches were a mixture of their two cultures.

Over all of this was the incessant banging of Peter (or Pietro, in honour of the great-great-grandfather), who was in his room giving it his all on the new electric drum set with lasers he had been given as a reward for passing the third year of high school.

I, personally, would have preferred a dog avatar. It made less noise and would have kept him out of the house. It would appear, however, that Pet was something of a musical prodigy and the drum set had been given in recognition of that genius.

«Start tidying up your drawings Maddy. If the table's not clear in five minutes, the whole lot is going in the bin».

It was an ancient ritual though, for Maddy never moved, intent as she was on solving a physics problem, and Mum, by the word *bin*, had practically cleared the table anyway. I already knew what was coming next and was ready.

«Philly, get the plates and start laying the table».

The synchronicity of our family would have allowed Jung to write a whole new treaty on the phenomenon. As soon as she had finished saying this, Dad invariably came home, announcing as he walked in, «Here I am», as if he were some diaphanous being conjured up out of thin air and not a 13-stone, 6-foot hulk of a man.

Although it seems strange, despite his physical stature, Dad was actually a professor of Philosophy, and one of the sweetest, most sensitive men on the planet.

As he entered, he kissed Mum like it was the first time, flew Maddy around the room like a ball, made a karate chop at Rupert, and stuck his fingers in his ears in a mock gesture of despair at the racket coming from Peter's room.

Finally, as we all knew he would, he turned on the 3D image projector on the wall facing the table.

A bleached blonde girl in a tight silver jumpsuit, who looked more like a lap dancer than a journalist, began in a sexy voice to inundate not only us, but probably thousands of others, with a barrage of chilling news stories which did little to stimulate the appetite.

The truth is, we were so used to hearing bad news that we would have been surprised if she had suddenly announced that Grouw March, the largest financier of the Confederation, had decided to come to the aid of the Yuti people of the Central Amazon and donate bales of freeze-dried wheat to ease the famine which had gripped the region for the last ten years.

There were no such reports, however, and so we started to eat.

«The epidemic, which has seen its first fatalities in the British land of the Federation, is reaching Zones 4, 5 and 6. Numerous cases have been detected in areas B, C and D in the districts of…».

«Health authorities recommend that…».

«A new epidemic – Mum said – every six months they terrorise us with this nonsense».

Dad gave a sort of grunt to indicate that he did not agree.

«This time it doesn't seem quite so stupid. Many are dying in Confederation 4 and the disease is spreading rapidly».

Mum looked at him

«Nobody has even the slightest idea of the cause and this is the biggest problem, nor of the way in which it is transmitted. People far removed from one another, with no form of contact, have been infected, and there are people who are seemingly immune living amongst the infected».

This comment seemed to go over Mum's head, for she was busy telling off Maddy for one of her tantrums.

Out of sheer love for Dad she asked, «What are the symptoms?».

«I don't know much about them. The papers mention pustules on the upper body which spread to the arms. Then you start sweating, lots and all the time. After that the tremors arrive, followed by hallucinations. You go crazy. Finally, you're seized by a raging fever and within 24 hours you're dead».

Dad took a mouthful of stew.

«The worst part is when people don't understand what's happening to them and they start to panic. Once that happens, they become aggressive and stop making any sense. In District B there have already been assaults on the supermarkets. People are stocking up on food and barricading themselves in their homes».

It was not an order, and neither was it a request, but Mum understood the message.

«With the four kids, we'd be better off stocking up on food before it runs out, epidemic or no epidemic».

«I think you're right. We could go tomorrow afternoon. We'll stock the house with cans, biscuits, supplement pills, freeze-dried food. That way we can rest a little easier and avoid getting caught in the stampede in the coming days».

I don't know why, but that seemingly harmless phrase filled me with a sense of dread, of something which at any moment could materialise before us, just as if the words of that sexy journalist had come out of the projector and manifested themselves right then and there, bringing that terrible virus to our table.

It is strange how, at times, our subconscious is able to pick up on danger from even the slightest of hints.

If, up until that point, I had never thought that all the bad things going on in the world: wars, illness, violence, could step over our threshold, in that moment I knew it was possible and that the door was likely to open at any minute.

The anxiety hit me like a blow to the stomach, right in the solar plexus. I looked around me and saw Maddy, Rupert, Peter with his blue quiff, Mum and Dad, but I felt alone, as if surrounded by ghosts.

Varick Street (New York City)

I am He who howls in the night;
I am He who moans in the snow;
I am He who hath never seen light;
I am He who mounts from below.

My car is the car of Death;
My wings are the wings of dread;

My breath is the north wind's breath;
My prey are the cold and the dead.

(H.P. Lovecraft, Psychopompos: A Tale in Rhyme)

Nights in the shelter were never-ending, hour after hour spent listening out for the slightest noise, the first sign of intruders.

Brief sleep was granted in the first light of dawn when the raids died down and the rats, tired and full, sought refuge in the recesses of the abandoned buildings and skyscrapers.

At the end of the day, she was no different from them.

After the fever and the catastrophe, she had wandered far and war, searching, hoping to find someone with whom to share, if not the overwhelming sense of loss she felt, the chance to recreate some sense of normality.

In the first week she had come across other humans, but had soon realised that she ought to stay away from them even more than the rats.

Crazed gangs roamed the streets spreading violence and terror. They would murder you in cold blood for as little as a half-eaten jar of expired jam or assault you without even pulling your knickers down.

Then, after those first few weeks, she had not met anyone else.

She had walked until her feet bled, far and wide down every street and every alley in the city.

She was looking for a safe place to stay, or safe enough, at least.

The outskirts and industrial areas were by now the territory of the rats and feral dogs, great, fearsome creatures that fought tooth and claw with the rats.

Manhattan, with its towering, mournful skyscrapers, turned out to be the best place to hide from the rats. Perhaps it was too windy for them. In any case, it offered a wealth of doorways, lift shafts and fire stairs which were easy to enclose and protect from the outside world.

She had chosen her hiding place because it was near the pond in the park.

Once upon a time, it had been home to magnificent swans.

Now, though, it was just an expanse of water in front of her house.

She had never thought to ask herself if the water was safe to drink or not, but she presumed that it was. In any case, she had never been sick and even if she had, she would have continued drinking it anyway.

During the day she wandered the streets in search of food, the evenings barricaded inside her shelter, her mind empty, in a daze.

That evening, however, the white bread had conjured up forgotten smells and memories, reminding her above all of the reason for which she now found herself in this place: the fever.

Bedford-Stuyvesant (New York City)

As planned, the following afternoon they had gone to pick up supplies. Her parents had managed to drag Peter along to help them carry the bags. She had been left in charge of Maddy and Rupert.

She didn't particularly mind, for she loved her little brother and sister, but that day she had been supposed to go out with Jack. It would have been an important outing, for rumours at school told her that there was a very good chance that Jack would have asked her to the end-of-year dance. Jack was only the most handsome, most desirable, nicest, most confident heartbreaker in her whole class.

She had never seen Jack again and did not know what had become of him.

She started to think up some game to play with the children, but Maddy took herself off to draw, while that natural pacifist Rupert decided to declare war on the lost land of the dinosaurs.

She threw herself down on the sofa and started to project images onto the wall.

Films, shows, interviews, everything, and more music than a New Year's Eve party.

As expected, she ended up on the breaking news, drawn morbidly to updates on the epidemic.

The news poured over her, like thousands of tiny pebbles: wars, insurrections, famine, the same ritual played out time after time in houses, while news of the epidemic rode over it all like a film played backwards.

Millions were dead, some in parts of the Confederation in which death was as old as the sunrise or rainfall, while others had been contaminated from the outside, no longer able to hide behind luxury and riches.

The epidemic did not respect boundaries of class or wealth.

The confident faces of doctors and scientists followed one after the other, all spouting empty words devoid of meaning, impossible to understand, cryptic pronouncements which bounced off the minds of those already overloaded with abstruse terms.

And behind it all the awful void of ignorance, of not knowing what would happen next.

The greatest scientists, the most brilliant minds, all aspiring to reach the pinnacle of knowledge, were now no better than the lowliest peasant of the Central Confederation.

Maddy, bent over on the floor, continued to draw, her tongue poking from her lips, totally absorbed in the task of setting her dreams down on paper.

She looked at her and for a moment believed that nothing could touch them and that the fever would never be able to find its way past the door which shut them off from the rest of the world: Maddy, Rupert and his battles, Pet and his blue quiff, Mum and Dad and their arguments over the mess in the bathroom and the crumbs left on the floor.

It was very late by the time they came back.

«It was like a battlefield, children! – her father said, as if he had just returned from an Interconfederate war – but we made it. Your mother has the fastest hands in New York when it comes to grabbing packets of chicos».

Mum smiled, but you could see she was tired

She looked frightened, as if the scrum at the supermarket had finally awakened her to the possibility of impending tragedy.

It is when a man perceives unknown dangers that the ancient instincts of his earliest ancestors resurface: gather food for the clan and batten down the hatches, like ants all rushing back to the nest with their load of breadcrumbs.

They ate chicos and beans from the can because Dad, laughing like a boy scout, thought that we might as well get used to it and that all their effort would at least seem worth it.

It was to be the first of many, for we never left the house again.

Varick Street (New York City)

She was thirsty. She took little sips of water and carefully closed the old plastic bottle.

How long had she been using it?

Did time have a meaning anymore?

Did the hours pass? Day, weeks, months?

Perhaps time no longer existed: only inside, and outside, depending on whether or not the rats were awake.

Perhaps time, which had once been under man's control, now belonged to the rats.

Once, near a bench on the outside, she had found a music box. A small white box beautifully decorated with silver and red designs.

She had opened it and inside, a solitary ballerina with her tutu slightly torn on one side, had begun her dance, round and round, always the same, accompanied by a sweet, monotonous melody.

She had started to cry. She watched the ballerina and cried, and as soon as it stopped she wound the key until the dance started up again, in time with her tears.

As she held the music box on that strange, deserted street, she had cried for her mother, for her father, for Rupert and for Peter.

She had cried for Maddy and her drawings, and she had cried for herself.

For the first time, her sorrow had freed itself from the sense of terrified stupor which, up until now, had suppressed it within her.

Then she had risen to her feet and closed the music box, leaving it there where she had found it, together with her desperation.

She took another sip, and another.

She was thirsty, so very thirsty.

Tiny drops of sweat began to cover her body.

She suddenly felt burst with joy.

She lay down on the mattress, touching herself to check the fever which was growing greater every minute, and waited.

Motherhood

The darkness was broken above her head by a bright purple light.

She tried to raise her hands to shield her eyes from the light, but realised that they would not move.

She did not feel as if they were tied down by anything; it was simply that her body would not obey the orders from her brain.

Noises from overhead sounded inside her head in an unknown language, broken words like gurgles or murmurs.

There were two small tubes in her nostrils. They felt detached from her, as if she was under anaesthetic, but she knew they were there.

Breathe, she had to breathe.

But she was already breathing. She needed to move, run, get up and run.

Two tall emaciated shadows appeared (or had they always been there?) from behind the light.

A strong odour struck her nostrils, brushing past the tubes and down her throat.

It was an odour she had smelled before, a disgusting smell, a smell like… snakes, enormous snakes.

It was the odour she had smelled once when, as a little girl, her father had taken her to visit the reptile show which was passing through their town.

Snakes? Where were they? Were they nearby?

She couldn't move, she had to breathe.

The figures bent over her, gurgling.

Then she screamed, and screamed, and screamed, as the light seemed to explode above her.

She woke up trembling and soaked in sweat. It was three on the morning, the usual nightmare.

She frantically reached for her nose to pull out the tubes but found only a drip of snot, probably the result of waking up so quickly. Her lips were covered in saliva and her whole body was bathed in a cold sweat.

As usual, it took her a moment to get her bearings and realise where she was and that it had all been a dream.

She got up, as she had been doing for months, with some difficulty, lifting her right leg first, and then raising herself to a seated position. She lifted the other leg and giving herself a push, staggered to her feet.

She went straight into the bathroom, used the toilet and washed her face and hands with cold water.

She felt better already. She looked at her reflection in the small rectangular mirror which hung over the sink. Her face seemed rounder than ever and her swollen lips appeared to grow beneath her nose like two pink donuts.

She stuck out her tongue. It would pass, soon it would pass and maybe she would be able once again to slip her feet back into her beloved black ballet slippers.

In the kitchen, she took a bottle of pear juice from the fridge and drank a glass.

The clock showed that it was about three-twenty.

Everything was as it should be, she could go back to bed for a good while.

She lay back down on her back and pulled up the sheet until it reached her chin, as she had been doing since she was little. It was the only way she was able to fall asleep; that and twirling her curls around her finger. The curl was no longer there, but she had the sheet.

She immediately fell into a deep and peaceful sleep.

The next morning, the sky was sombre and clear as only October mornings are.

After having breakfast and getting dressed, she sat down on the sofa to watch the early news on TV.

She hopped between all the available channels, finally settling on the last episode of an old series. It seemed like the perfect morning for a walk and a bit of shopping.

No sooner had she stepped out the door than Mrs. Milss, her next-door neighbour, gave her the usual wave.

«Deeeeear, you're more beautiful than ever, none of us can wait! Enjoy your walk. If you need anything just call and I'll be right over».

She did not doubt this last comment one bit, for Mrs. Milss would have walked through fire to stick her nose in other people's business. As for her being more beautiful than ever, she very much doubted it, not to mention that the only *we* in their two adjacent bungalows were her and Mrs. Milss.

She walked quickly, despite her condition.

Even if everything else suggested otherwise, she was delighted with the state in which she found herself.

From the very beginning and with breathtaking speed, she had felt an enormous and very positive change within her. It was as if her whole being was utterly absorbed in preparation for what was to come.

For months she had tried to hide, but then, when it was no longer possible, she had happily conceded to revealing herself.

A strong, decisive signal in her brain told her that she should share it with someone.

There was Mrs. Milss, but she wasn't really anybody worth sharing it with, and besides, by now she was practically part of the Project.

She ventured out to the local shops a few times, but the feeling of heaviness that morning had increased and she felt that at any minute she would double over.

She decided to go straight back inside.

Once home, she lay down on the sofa, her eyes open, waiting to experience any emotion.

She had not the slightest idea of what she was supposed to do, nor of what would happen, but she did not feel afraid. She had dutifully obeyed all of the strange rules imposed by her brain. The message which came to her now was «wait», «lie down», «keep calm», «take deep breaths».

She might have been lying on the sofa for ten minutes or ten hours (it didn't matter, after all, she obeyed the rules) when she suddenly felt a swift, decisive movement.

A sharp but bearable pain seared through her vagina up towards her uterus.

She breathed in and out slowly, as the rules dictated and raised herself slightly, resting her head and shoulders on the arm rest.

She was every so slightly dilated. Instinctively, she opened her legs and pulled off her knickers, a rush of yellowish water and with the water, or just after, she didn't know, it appeared.

A great, green, soft lizard with round eyes; yes round, huge and green, a lighter green than its skin.

The little one looked at her, drinking her in with its great round eyes. The long, graceful tail wagged joyfully.

With one hand she lifted it up and with the other began to caress its head, enjoying the feel of its smooth cool skin.

The little one wriggled up into the space beneath her breasts. With a sigh, she threw her head back and laughed.

Wail

Literally translated, the name *Chupacabra* means "goat sucker". It has attracted the attention of ufologists, biologists and cryptozoologists. Legend has it that this creature is armed with a mouth which is able to penetrate the flesh and bones of its victims, injecting a substance which brings on rigor mortis. Piercing three holes near the jugular, the creature uses this supposed mouth to drain its victim's blood, cauterising the wound in the same instant, and removing internal organs and other tissues. Strangely, the victim's blood does not coagulate.

The figure of the chupacabra is often associated with the frequent slaughter of animals in Mexico and with cases where animals are found dead or mutilated under mysterious circumstances.

The most frequent description is of an upright but slightly hunched creature, which moves in leaps and bounds over the rooftops, leaving behind a three-toed paw print (the chupacabra's actual footprint has yet to be ascertained, for at the site of the attacks there are often prints which are not identifiable with any animal known to man). Their limbs are said to be long, ending in three articulated toes. They have a long face and narrow red eyes, two holes in place of nostrils, small pointed ears and spines, like a crocodile, running down their back and head. There are also those who claim that instead of scales, their bodies are covered in long bristly fur.

These "scales" are supposedly able to vibrate, producing a strange sound, which witnesses say is accompanied by an unpleasant smell. One characteristic of the chupacabra is that it walks over the rooftops of houses. It is said to make a terrible noise on the corrugated iron roofs of certain houses in Mexico, Chile, and other parts of the world where the creature has been sighted. The "noise" of the chupacabra has been described as terrible, high-pitched cry.

It is said that the creature is between 60 and 180cm tall.

Some witnesses have stated that it possesses paranormal powers.

Its capacity to read minds has frequently been reported, as has its ability to communicate with humans telepathically.

Witnesses also report having been hypnotised, while others say that the Chupacabra is able to change colour and, therefore, camouflage itself in the same way that a chameleon does. There are people who are convinced that it walks amongst us and accompanies us in our daily lives, but that we are unable to see it.

Witnesses report that it is able to levitate and fly on currents of air, reaching speeds of up to 250km per hour. They also report that the chupacabra possesses superhuman strength and is capable of both cutting through animal pens and cages with great precision and pulling them apart. They seem to be able to enter animal enclosures without causing any damage, almost as if they had passed straight through them, or materialised inside by traversing some sort of portal.

Inversely, this animal is sometimes described as being similar to a canine, or marsupial, with wings on its back (described as a winged dog), a hairless body, pointed fangs, and claws.

Often, sightings of the chupacabra occur after UFO sightings, and always in the same area.

San Antonio (Texas)

Ellis's farm was built right in the centre of his family's vast lands.

From its solid central farmhouse it was possible to survey the entire surrounding estate.

Ellis had been born there, just like his father, and his grandfather before him. Four generations of robust Texans had sweated and toiled under the burning sun.

Decades ago, his ancestors had emigrated from Ireland in search of fertile land to till.

They had found it there, in that corner of the world so far removed from the damp green hills of the Thuanna.

And Irish they had remained: short, stocky, strong, and as stubborn as mules. They were great workers, great drinkers, with red hair and skin darkened by the many years spent labouring outside under an unforgiving sun.

Time, however, had also changed the proud Groves family.

Ellis had been left alone on the farm, for none of his three children possessed the old passion which made a farmer like Ellis take a handful of earth and let it fall through his fingers to see if it was moist enough for planting.

His eldest son was a doctor in the north of the country.

His daughter taught history at the University of Alabama, while the youngest had enrolled and was now an officer in the Air Force.

Ellis, however, still held out some hope, for just as the earth does not die, for an Irishman there was no such thing as dying far from home.

They would return.

It was one of those typical Texas evenings; the sky was clear, with cirrus clouds on the horizon, and no breeze.

The silence which surrounded the house seemed to create a vacuum.

There was no sound, no birdsong, no lowing of cattle, no dog barking, and too early even for the howl of the coyotes which came out shortly after sunset.

The sheep fixed the horizon in silence from inside their great enclosure.

Ellis took a seat in the rocking chair on his front porch; just time for one more beer, maybe even two.

It was not as if there was much to do after the animals had been bedded down for the night and so, like the sheep, he fixed his eyes on the horizon and watched the red sunset.

Every day was the same.

It was just as he was about to open his second can of beer that he heard the sound. At least, he thought it was a sound.

In reality, it was somewhere between a sharp shriek and the wail of a dog in heat.

The sheep shifted in their pen, moving in waves like a sea of white wool.

The two dogs whimpered.

Then all was silence again.

Ellis got to his feet and, narrowing his eyes, tried to see beyond the fir tree fence which surrounded his house.

Perhaps it had been the cry of a large owl, or an animal caught in the snare of some poacher, or one hundred other things besides.

Strange clouds had suddenly appeared on the horizon, clouds which did not resemble anything Ellis had seen in all his 70 years. They were great, soft, shifting clouds like enormous snowflakes, surrounded by a greenish pink light which shone between openings in the formation and seemed to emanate from a place far away in the sky.

It could have been the beginning of a tornado.

There was another sharp cry, this time close by.

He heard the bark of the dogs, followed again by a frightened whimper.

If it was some damned coyote out before the sunset in search of food to silence his grumbling tummy, he would soon see to it.

Going back inside, he took his hunting rifle and loaded it with pellets.

He thought to himself: «Come on, come a little closure, you'll see».

He bounded out of the house and headed towards the sheep enclosure.

He found them all huddled along its edge, paralysed, the mothers standing in front of the lambs as if to protect them.

What he then saw in the middle of the pen made his blood run cold: four sheep lay dead, their bellies swollen and soft, as if empty inside.

He moved closer. There was no blood, not so much as a drop, no marks or wounds on the body. The next was turned to one side: there were three puncture marks along the jugular.

He touched the stomachs of the dead sheep, they were like empty bags.

Whatever it had been, it had drained the sheep's internal organs, leaving them limp and empty like plastic bags.

He wiped the sweat from his brow.

The dogs had retreated to their kennels and despite their size, were now reduced to whimpering puppies.

The clouds continued to gather on the horizon and flashed brightly and often.

«It must be a tornado – he thought to himself – one of those ones that carry off houses like autumn leaves. Perhaps some hungry lynx sensed it was coming and decided to feed early».

He did not wish to dwell on the empty stomachs.

He never thought about the impossible. Everything, sooner or later, had an explanation, which was enough to convince a good Christian like him.

However, he now no longer wished to stay on the porch and decided that it was better to go back inside and get some sleep (tornado permitting).

His room was at the end of the corridor.

He had started sleeping in that room after the death of his wife Amy and the departure of his children.

It was a small, cosy room, with a beautifully wrought iron bedstead.

When she was still alive, Amy had referred to it as the guest room.

The only thing was that in forty years of marriage, they had never had a single guest.

After undressing and taking off his boots, he lay down.

Sleep took him immediately, like an unexpected fog.

A voice in his head said to him: «Sleep, stay still, sleep».

He heard the sound softly through the fog, his body seized by exhaustion.

There was a scuffling on the tin roof, like someone hopping on one leg.

The voice in his head seemed to say: «Sleep, don't get up, I'm hungry».

He turned towards the window and thought he saw a great bird brush past the glass.

An eagle? He was sleeping, it was just a dream.

The scuffling returned, accompanied by the faint sound of something knocking on the tin roof.

He heard the cry, louder and more shrill this time. It pierced the air and seemed to wake him.

«Don't move, I'm hungry».

He remained there, immobile, listening to the small footsteps which now ran along the guttering.

When he realised that the creature was there it was too late.

It was just a second, a mere moment in time.

He felt raised into the air then sucked back down again, almost gently, without force.

Two small red eyes were watching him. Where its nose should have been were two heaving nostrils.

Was it a smile that he saw as a long thin tongue like that of snake slid out of its mouth?

The fog, now thicker than ever, wrapped him in terrifying darkness and he felt nothing more.

Play With Me

For I am every dead thing…
… He ruin'd me, and I am re-begot
Of absence, darkness, death – things which are not.

(JOHN DONNE, *A Nocturnal upon St. Lucy's Day*).

Wednesday, 12 October

The Ford station wagon stopped in front of the green wooden gate. The house was the one that Pegott had always dreamed of and he was proud to have found it for her.

It hadn't been easy, for Pegott always found something that was wrong with it or missing.

It may have been that there was one room too few, the room next to the kitchen to use as a laundry, for example; or that the ceilings in the rooms were not the right height.

The road was too near or the shops too far away. Once, believe it or not, she had not liked the face of the vendor. The poor man had had a crooked nose, which she declared to be a sign of dishonesty.

This house, on the other hand, they had happened to find by chance, as is often the case with the events and people which alter the course of your life. Chance is the one thing you can truly count on in life.

It was that afternoon that they had decided to go and buy a new coat for Heliott. The little boy was growing before their eyes and his arms and legs seemed to get longer by the day.

They had an excellent range of boyswear at the shopping centre on the new superhighway: fun but well-made clothes at an affordable price.

They were on their way when Pegott, who was smoking a cigarette, saw it.

«This one Paul, this one I really like».

He was driving, but he understood immediately what she meant by *this one*.

The following day they contacted the agency and made an appointment to go and view it.

Paul knew that he could have written a cheque on the spot without even seeing it. Once Pegott made up her mind on instinct, not only was it impossible to get her to change it, but more often than not, it turned out to be the right decision.

Helliott pressed his nose to the car window and screwed up his eyes behind his milk-bottle glasses to take a better look.

The high sycamore trees hid most of the front porch from view, but he could still see the closed windows on the first floor.

«Do you like it Hel?».

Pegott never asked questions, for she had no need for approval.

This question was simply part of an affectionate ritual she liked to keep up with her son.

«Your room is on the first floor. As a matter of fact, all the bedrooms are on the first floor. On the ground floor we have the dining area and living room».

She had liked the division of these two rooms, for symbolically, it raised her one more step up the social ladder.

A great blackbird suddenly flew out of a sycamore and landed on the sill of one of the three windows. It started to turn its head from one side to the other, examining the three new guests with curiosity.

It was at the exact moment that followed that a great whirling gust of wind blew up out of nowhere.

As if on cue, yellow leaves began falling from the trees and twirling through the air, dancing round and round each other as they fell to the ground.

A minute? Ten minutes? An hour? Timed seemed not to matter. Then, as quickly as it had started, the wind died down again and the air was filled with a quiet calm, as if waiting for something.

Jumping up, Jack opened the car door and got out.

«I think we ought to get out and start unloading something. We can't sit staring at it from forever, it's our house now».

Pegott opened the boot and started to take out various packages. They had brought only the essentials to get them through the first two or three days until the removal company brought the rest of their things.

As it was, there wasn't all that much to bring, as the house was already furnished. As the existing furniture was a lot better than their own, they had decided to leave it the way it was and sell their old furniture to a dealer.

They walked into the large entrance hall. The high ceiling lit up the room through a glass skylight overhung by the tips of the tallest sycamores.

A brass hat stand and a large walnut wardrobe took up one wall, while on the other was a beautiful chest, which also served as a table for the telephone.

The entrance hall led into a corridor neatly separating the various rooms. On the right was the kitchen and utility room, on the left the reception room with large sofas upholstered in nineteenth-century dark green velvet and the living room with a crystal table and eight seats.

Pegott headed straight for the kitchen with two large boxes in her arms containing food for the fridge.

«Jack, bring me the boxes with the plates and cutlery, and the one with the saucepans, I'll start organising things. While I'm doing that, why don't you take Hel upstairs and show him his room? And remember that he needs to have a shower before he comes down for supper».

Helliott followed his father upstairs.

The air was heavy, close, thick with dust and strange smells.

His father whistled as he climbed the stairs and appeared not to notice.

At the first landing, on his left, was a small window. At least, it looked like a window, but it was walled up and covered with a wooden shutter.

He felt a breath on his back as he walked past.

Everything felt closed-off and there were strange odours (but of what?), years of dust, a flash of light.

Once his father had shown him his room, he left and Helliott sat down on the bed and looked around.

It was a huge room, too big for him.

One the wall facing the bed stood two imposing wardrobes with finely carved doors.

Under the window was a desk and everywhere shelves filled with books, dolls, wooden toys, and even four marionettes as large as a child. Pegott had found it all decidedly elegant and had decided to leave the furnishings as they were, including the toys.

Helliott grimaced, he was too big for those sorts of games.

The good thing (for it is always important to look for the positives) was that no one would have been able to tease him about it, for Helliott did not have any friends, not a single one.

The marionette with a monkey face was looking at him with an amused air so Hel stuck out his tongue at it.

A rustle, sensations , a smell (of what?)

Resigned to the fact that he would he would have to take a shower, he made his way towards the bathroom.

The monkey rapidly lifted its arm, moving the strings which held it, turned its head, then fell still again, its glass eyes staring in wonder as the door to the bathroom closed behind the boy.

After he had washed, Hel went down to the kitchen. Pegott had made a supper of ham on toast, chocolate hazelnut spread on sweet bread, and slightly runny pudding.

They were all hungry and so they cleared their plates.

«Let's go and have some fun in our new garden», his father said, lifting Helliott onto his shoulders.

His parents sat down on the first step of the porch and he wrapped himself like a kitten around their feet.

The air was still warm, with that humidity which comes with early autumn evenings.

A carpet of yellowed leaves covered the still green grass beneath the sycamores.

Rustling, silence, rustling.

Small silver balls shot through the grass.

A strong smell.

He rubbed his eyes beneath his thick glasses and looked up at his father.

He wore a satisfied smile, with a glass of milk in one hand and the other on his mother's shoulder.

Was he imagining it? The balls returned to bounce around the grass, quick as lightening.

At the bottom of the garden near the washing line, the see-saw was moving with a light, regular movement, creaking ever so slightly.

It was his father who took him up to bed.

He tucked him tightly, arranged the pillow under his head, and gave him the usual affectionate cuff which was his idea of a cuddle.

«No comics tonight, straight to sleep».

He took off his glasses for him and set them down on the bedside table.

Behind him, the marionette nodded its head is if in agreement.

As always, with his glasses removed, the world around him became a haze so that objects lost their solidity and took on a soft, undulating edge.

He held is breath as he saw a shadow moving behind his father's broad shoulders.

He appeared not to notice.

«Good night Helliott».

«Good night Daddy».

As soon as his father had left the room, closing the door behind him, Helliott wriggled deeper under the covers and, just to be sure, covered the gap left behind with his pillow.

There was something in the room.

No, not something, someone.

He couldn't see anything, but it was as if there was a crack in the air, an invisible body which filled the space in between.

He felt a gentle breathing above him.

The curls at the nape of neck moved ever so slightly, as if disturbed by a light breeze.

Someone (something) was moving around his bed.

A smell.

A feeling.

«Alone».

The word exploded inside his head like a sudden flash of lightening.

«Who are you?».

«Alone».

A wave of pain and fear overcame and filled every last space in his brain.

Whoever was watching him as he hid beneath the covers was more afraid than him.

«I'm Helliott».

«Alone».

The air was chilled, still, as if waiting for something.

He thought for a moment that it might have left, as if it was normal that whatever sort of apparition it was had entered his room only to leave again. But Helliott could tell that it had neither come nor gone away: it was there *alone* in that house. He peaked out from beneath the covers, even if he knew that without his glasses he would not have been able to see a thing.

To risk stretching out his arm to pick them up from the bedside table was out of the question.

Through his blurry vision the room seemed to him the same as before.

Perhaps just the funny monkey-faced marionette seemed to have moved slightly.

He slid back under the protection of the covers and sleep overtook him in an instant with the same sense of oblivion that he had experienced when he had his adenoids out and they had covered his face with a strange mask.

With sleep came the images, clear, organised, fluid, as if in a story.

It was then, as he slept, that he understood what had happened.

As he slept, his whole mind concentrated on preserving the images that came to him.

A land (no, a world Helliott, no, not a world, a place Helliott), strange and far away.

Endless lands of brilliant white sand, two enormous suns which gave of a measureless heat.

Airplanes (no Helliott, not airplanes, shuttles, modules, Helliott) which darted about without rest. Enormous metal spiders digging in the sand.

Images came to him in the silence of the white sand.

Then came a different scene, a child (look carefully, Helliott, a child?) walking on a lawn. The lawn belonged to his house and the scared child was walking towards it. The final image, crystal clear, like a photograph: two thin tubes protruding from a small pointed nose.

After that he saw nothing more and slipped into a deep and dreamless sleep.

He turned over and curled up into a foetal position, with his fists tucked beneath his chin.

Something gently made room for itself beside him: the mattress folded into a slight dip, as if bearing the lightest of weights.

Thursday 13 October

Fantasmi
Era l'ora innominabile della notte
In cui le illusioni in un nembo delirante
Intorno al silenzioso dormiente, ondeggiano
E si muovono furtive nelle sue visioni inconsce

H.P. Lovecraft

The next morning, Helliott woke late. His head felt heavy, as if weighed down by an iron helmet which dug into his temples.

Either way, he did not have to go to school because Mummy Peg still had to sign him up and talk to the Headmaster.

He could take it easy.

He slipped on an old tracksuit and went downstairs for breakfast.

The smell of hot donuts, his mother's speciality, overtook him when he was only four steps down.

His father had also taken a day off work (he sold steel rods for industrial machines, which was always exactly what he said when people asked him about his job).

He was seated at the table regaling Peggott with tales of their new home.

«The owner of the agency, Mr. Filly, told me that it was built by an English engineer more than 100 years ago. He really knew what he was doing, the sort of builder you don't find these days», he moved his arms as if to draw an imaginary line in the air.

«He built the house on an east-west axis, but with the windows and porch facing south. It was designed according to the layout of old English manors: in the winter it is warmed by the low sun, and in the summer it only enjoys the sun in the morning and the evening. Ah, Americans don't build houses like this one; they build willy-nilly, without skill or precision. Americans aren't capable of designing a house according to the angle of the sun or the wind, Americans…».

«Jack, we're Americans».

Peggott put another donut on his plate and he nibbled it as if to say, on this occasion at least, that he was sorry not to have been born European.

His mother kissed his forehead and told him to sit down next to his father, serving him a large mug of sweet apple cordial and three donuts.

«Tomorrow we'll go and put your name down at your new school, then you'll see how many friends you'll make!».

«And now that you have a nice big room and even a garden, you'll be able to invite them round to do their homework and play», his father added.

To be honest, Helliott had his doubts.

He had never had a friend, or even enemies for that matter.

It was worse than that, for the other children his age usually just ignored him, as if he was an invisible child.

No one had ever invited him to play, either at school or at their house.

The only time that Peggott had organised a birthday party for him, just Molly Kemp had shown up, dragging along her sulky daughter Linda.

Of the other people invited, no one else had come.

Not that Helliott minded, he got on just fine on his own. He loved playing with his robots or toy soldiers and made up exciting stories for them.

He did not like playing football or basketball and rugby frightened him. His bicycle, on the other hand, was an excellent companion on long rides around the neighbourhood.

Sometimes, on Sundays, he and his father rode to the park.

There, he bought him candyfloss and they sat down on the bench to read, his father the paper and he his favourite comic.

He loved those Sunday mornings so much that it didn't matter to him that he had no friends.

As soon as he had finished his donuts he went into the garden to explore. The air was still warm and the garden, at that time of the morning, well-lit and inviting.

He got his bike out of the garage and rode up and down the small avenue which led to the gate.

He soon got bored, as the road was not long enough. He did not have permission to explore the neighbourhood yet.

He sat down on the swing and swung back and forth. It was fun to watch the branches of the trees close-up, then far away, like a dance.

He closed his eyes to enjoy the sensation of the swing and pushed harder.

«Lovely».

«There it was again, that voice».

Sensations, smells, rustling.

«Lovely. Can you move that thing with your mind?».

Helliott felt obliged to answer.

«I'm the one moving it. It's called a swing. I'm pushing it. You see, like this».

And he gave it a hard push.

«Lovely. Can you move the swing thing with your mind?».

It was just a split second, but before Helliott even had time to answer, the swing shook so violently that the ropes rotated in their hinges and the boy went flying, coming down to land two metres away on the grass.

A frightened scream ripped through his mind.

«Fear».

The rest of the day passed like any other, utterly boring.

Neither Peggott, Jack nor Helliott had any conception of monotony. On the contrary, they found it reassuring.

Not even the new house could shake them out of their usual routine.

After only a day, it seemed as if they had always lived there, for they behaved the same way, kept to the same schedule, so that what was new to them soon came to be completely natural.

Helliott was even quieter than usual.

Any moment, he expected to hear the voice again, some sign, a movement. He wanted to know, to understand; no, actually he did not want to understand.

To know something was enough for him to accept it. Beyond that he chose not to ask.

It had been the same when the other children teased him, avoided him, laughed behind his back.

He had knowingly sought out solitude, which was the only friend he ever needed and certainly suited him better than the loud chatter of the other children.

Peggott, with diligence and planning, had already unpacked the objects in the boxes they had brought with them, which now lay folded in a pile near the front door, ready to be taken out to the dustbin.

«Tomorrow I'll take you in to see your new school».

«Ok Mummy».

No protest, no tantrum: the sooner he met the new kids the better.

That way, they could dismiss him as an idiot and cast him aside before he'd even got to know them, and he could go back to his old routine.

They had supper in front of a TV quiz show which his parents had been watching for the last ten years.

During the whole of a dull, dark, and soundless day in the autumn of the year, when the clouds hung oppressively low in the heavens [...] It was a mystery all insoluble; nor could I grapple with the shadowy fancies that crowded upon me as I pondered.

But the shadow was vague, and formless, and indefinite, and was the shadow neither of man nor of God – neither God of Greece, nor God of Chaldaea, nor any Egyptian God. And the shadow rested upon the brazen doorway, and under the arch of the entablature of the door, and moved not, nor spoke any word, but there became stationary and remained.

(Edgar Allan Poe, The Fall of the House of Usher / Shadow)

«Go straight to sleep Helliott – his mother said – tomorrow I'm going to wake you up early so that we can go and meet your new friends».

Even she said this without much enthusiasm, as if she was also aware of how it would turn out.

«Ok».

Helliott made his way towards the stairs.

A sense of deep despair tightened around his chest.

The solitude of his condition crushed him like a stone which had fallen silently, out of nowhere, on his head.

Everything to which he held faithful, games with his toy soldiers, bicycle rides, complicated jigsaw puzzles, card games with his father, now all appeared empty, an immense void, a vortex of nothingness through which he could not see the other side.

He turned around to look at his parents, Peggott who was tidying up the kitchen, and Daddy Jack who was fixing the mixer.

He looked at them and felt as if it was the last time that he would ever see them.

He quickly looked away and carried on upstairs, for there was nothing else to do.

He turned on the small bedside lamp.

He bent down to undo his shoelaces.

The monkey winked at him and swung a paw back and forth.

It didn't seem strange to him.

The air was dense, clammy, almost like rubber.

He felt as if he was moving inside an enormous gum bubble.

Small rustlings here and there, sensations, the air moving, like rubber, then light to the touch, somewhere above his shoulders.

«I'm here. Come».

He said these words to himself, knowing that they would be enough.

«I'm scared», the voice said in his mind, like always.

«I'm waiting for you, come».

There were things around us and about of which I can render no distinct account – things material and spiritual – heaviness in the atmosphere – a sense of suffocation – anxiety – and, above all, that terrible state of existence which the nervous experience when the senses are keenly living and awake, and meanwhile the powers of thought lie dormant. A dead weight hung upon us. It hung upon our limbs – upon the household furniture – upon the goblets from which we drank; and all things were depressed, and borne down thereby…

(Edgar Allan Poe, *Shadow*).

He sat down on the bed with the pillow propped up behind him. He didn't take off his glasses, even though he knew that what was coming he would have been able to see regardless. Together. Silence.

There are some qualities – some incorporate things,
That have a double life, which thus is made
A type of that twin entity which springs
From matter and light, evinced in solid and shade.
There is a twofold Silence – sea and shore –
Body and soul. One dwells in lonely places,
Newly with grass o'ergrown; some solemn graces,

Some human memories and tearful lore,
Render him terrorless: his name's «No More».
He is the corporate Silence: dread him not!
No power hath he of evil in himself;
But should some urgent fate (untimely lot!)
Bring thee to meet his shadow (nameless elf,
That haunteth the lone regions where hath trod
No foot of man), commend thyself to God!

(EDGAR ALLAN POE, *Silence*)

The images appeared in his mind, covered in a grey fog at first, then, like a lens which gradually comes into focus, ever clearer and more distinct.

Great wastes of sand, a great sun which burned the eyes with its white-hot heat and, next to it, low in the sky, another sun, red and much smaller.

Sand, sand, light, heat.

Small creatures moving on strange machines which looked like enormous metallic spiders.

Thirst, thirst which burned and dried the throat, spreading throughout the whole body. Strong these feelings of his were: thirst and heat.

Small tubes which entered the face by small holes, not the nose, but small holes, a feeling of wellbeing, of something assuaging the thirst.

And once again, he saw the great ship, imposing and alone, as it took flight in deep space, passing by suns before entering into the stellar darkness, the bursting light of hyperspace.

Another moment and then a planet appeared, surrounded by white clouds and partly covered in water.

The blue of the great watery expanse consoled his heart.

Dozens of tiny blue craft, like birds in search of food, broke away from the mothership and shot through the sky above the planet of blue water.

Joy, rapture, euphoria.

Sensations.

«Fear».

He saw a small darting spacecraft smothered in red flames, falling in a deadly spin, through the sky towards the planet, piercing the white clouds in its path.

Flashes, impact, pain, fear, nothing, emptiness.

Helliott lifted his head and the images dispersed.

The monkey watched him with its dead glass eyes.

It was then that he saw it.

It was standing right in front of his bed.

A tiny being, not much taller than him.

It had an elongated head and two small eyes above its noseless nostrils. Its mouth cut across one side of its face to the other, the corners slightly turned down.

Long thin arms hung still by its side. From the left shoulder almost down to the pubic bone was a great slash, out of which poured slowly, softly, a thick white liquid.

«You're dead».

«I mean, you fell and now you're dead».

The voice in his head only replied «Dead».

It seemed to Helliott that he did not know the meaning of the word.

«Dead means that you're no longer alive, that you don't exist anymore».

The creature's eyes narrowed slightly and the mouth seemed to smile.

«You can see me, therefore I'm here».

Then, the creature curled up at the boy's feet and took his hand with his own, long, bendy fingers touching his skin. He squeezed it slightly and brought it up to his face.

«Alone».

«I'm alone too».

This contact brought about in him a sense of peace and tranquillity, a sweetness he had never known before, not even when he was small and Peggott used to rock him to sleep.

He felt that he would never need to be anywhere else or with anyone else.

He climbed down from the bed and sat beside the creature.

Small coloured spheres started to dance all around them as the room filled with every colour imaginable.

Helliott raised an arm and caressed the elongated head, a warm rush of love washing over him like a wave.

«Play with me».

The spheres multiplied and gave off flashes of fluorescence. The monkey clapped its hands in silent applause.

They looked for him for days, in every corner of the house, in the garden, spreading to search the surrounding area, the terror mounting inside them.

The grief over the loss of Helliott destroyed Peggott's mind and closed Jack in the silence of a lucid madness.

After their deaths, when the house had been sold, one of the builders working on the restorations opened up the space behind the wooden shutter on the stairs.

The two skeletons were there.

One of them, with a strangely elongated head, was embracing the other with a long, emaciated arm.

The Menhir

Lenda

In the nineteenth century, the French novelist Gustave Flaubert wrote: «Carnac has had more nonsense written about it than it has standing stones», thereby confirming that the endless attempts to give an explanation to the presence of the megalithic monuments were largely based on conjectures and individual fancy, often without proper foundation. Today, thanks to scientific research, we have more information by which to evaluate the stones. Notwithstanding, it is a phenomenon which still remains largely shrouded in mystery. If the initial explanation, preserved in the funerary meaning of the names assigned to the various alignments, was probably connected to the traditional worship of ancestral spirits and their tombs, following the arrival of people devoted to agriculture, the stones became absorbed into the cult of nature and the worship of celestial phenomena.

It has been noted that the alignment of Kerlascan is positioned towards the rising of the sun at the equinoxes, while that of Kermario faces the rising of the sun at the summer solstice. Ménec, meanwhile, occupies an intermediary position. Other rows of menhirs supposedly relate to the rising of the sun on important dates in the farming calendar: 4 February (the birth of the new plants), 6 May (flowering), 8 August (harvest time), 8 November (planting).

According to Professor Alexander Thom of Oxford University, the megalithic complex at Carnac is an enormous Neolithic "astronomical clock" designed to identify the periods of planting and ploughing through observation of the lunar cycle. He noted that the rows of menhirs were spaced according to a precise set of distances, corresponding to 8, 10, 12 and 14 megalithic yards (1 yard = 81.6cm) and that at the point in which one group meets another, the shape of the circles incorporates "Pythagoric" triangles. The Carnac Stones are arranged according to advanced principles of mathematics and geometry, through which it is possible to carry out astronomical observations of a highly complex nature. If the same purpose seems to have been served by the comparatively small megalithic temple at Stonehenge, why was it deemed necessary to extend the stones at Carnac over a space of more than 8 kilometres and a total of 5000 menhirs? The experts' answer is that the coast of Morbihan is home to an astronomical clock of gigantic proportions with the highest possible number of reference points for carrying out observations. This clock was designed with the scope of "capturing" the greatest amount of energy possible through the sheer number of skyward facing stones. It is said that persons of a highly sensitive nature can still feel strong electrical currents along the avenues of stones. Other researchers have rejected such explanations, stating that it is impossible to know for sure that the stones at Carnac had a precise astronomical function or that they were originally connected to the cult of the dead. For the same reason, these same scientists have affirmed that the religious function of the stones could originate in the cult of fertility related to livestock or similar.

Around 10,000 B.C., a group of Mesolithic fishermen and hunter-gatherers settled on the small islands in the Bay of Quiberon in southern Brittany, which face the celebrated megalithic sites of Carnac and Locmariaquer. The islands of Teviec and Hoédic, in particular, became the site of villages formed of huts and encircled with large stones.

The availability of great granite masses and the probable arrival of people from the outside, bringing with them a religion based on the cult of the dead, gave rise to the oldest megalithic complexes known in Europe: both simple dolmen and tombs formed of rooms, galleries and corridors constructed beneath long earth barrows.

In the year 10,150, the Di Aniuit clan ruled over the entire region.

Lenda was bent over, gathering Mut's herb.

She was enveloped in a grey cape, with the hood pulled down over her face to shield her eyes.

Drops of sweat trickled down her back.

The great sun beat down mercilessly on the whole expanse of land.

She moved quickly, working with the skill of someone who had done so for years, pulling up the stems right at the base, without touching the roots.

New Mut plants would grow again within a few days.

She was hot and soaked with sweat, but never thought for one moment about stopping.

Lenda did not belong to the clan.

Lenda was an outcast, without name or land, something less than a slave or animal; she was one of Mut's mistakes.

The basket she kept tied to her waist was now full and so she decided that it was time to take the herbs back to Di U An, the medicine woman, who was waiting for her in the hut.

She stood up and straightened her back, looking over towards the menhir.

The menhir was the strength of the clan and the fertility of the earth.

It had been there since long before Lenda was born, since before the clan arrived in those lands, long before any other thing had lived there.

At least, this is what Di U An and the warriors of Di Aiunit had told her.

Lenda did not believe it was possible, because somebody must have erected the menhir, but she was careful not to say so, for her life would be worth less than a flea on Di U An's dog if she did.

The whole surface of the monolith was covered in mysterious graffiti.

Sometimes, although she was mad to think so, she had the impression that if she'd moved closer to it she would have been able to decipher its meaning.

But no one was permitted to go any closer than ten steps, least of all an outcast like her.

Di U An's hut was situated at the far end of the village, right on the bank of the torrent and so to reach it, Lenda had to walk past all the other huts in the village.

At that time of day, the entire clan was outside, engaged in various forms of labour. The warriors were sat in a circle telling stories of their ancestors.

No one looked up as she walked past, for according to their laws, Lenda, Mut's mistake, did not exist.

By now it did not matter anymore, quite the opposite. Sometimes it was good to be invisible.

There had been a time, however, when she did not understand and their attitude had upset her. As a little girl, still unsteady on her feet, she would run after the women and children, pulling on their cloaks and banging their shins, if only to make them look at her.

They all just brushed her aside like an insect. It was at that point that Di U An left her herbs and came to drag her into the hut.

«Lenda, you must not touch the Di Aniut. The wrath of Mut will come down upon you when you least expect it and the great warrior will cut you into pieces so small that the dogs will gobble you up without even stopping to chew».

Then she took her in her arms and sighing, kissed her face.

She took the child to the mirror and said:

«Look at yourself, child. Behold the error of Mut. Can you see it? You do not belong to the clan, you do not belong to the land, you do not belong to anything». She put her nut-brown face up against that of the child.

Lenda did not understand anything of those words back then, but just looked at the two faces in amazement.

Lenda's skin was as pale as ice, white too her fine hair, her eyes two enormous empty orbs with two sky blue pinheads at their centre.

It was only afterwards that she understood and never tried to touch anyone ever again.

Di U An sewed her the grey cloak which covered her from head to toe. Besides shielding her from the frightened gaze of the clan, it protected her from the far greater threat of the enormous sun whose rays, on more than one occasion, had left burns on her skin.

Di U An loved the child. It had been her who had found her and first brought her to the village.

It was likely that if Di had not taken her in her arms and carried her back to the village wrapped in her shawl, the child would have been burnt as an offering to Mut.

But it was Di U An who knew how to heal, and so she was a sacred figure.

The eyes of Di U An saw what others could not and in her wisdom she saw visions which no warrior, woman or sorcerer could ever dream of.

Her mind had travelled to places far away, far beyond the constellation of Orion and the great dying stars at the end of the galaxy.

Di U An now awaited the moment when the child would be able to see for herself and share her knowledge.

When Lenda was five years old something happened which changed the course of her life.

After months of drought, during which the sun had dried up the earth and left both people and animals gasping for water, a great storm arrived that was so intense and so prolonged, that the entire village was transformed into a lake of mud.

Only the menhir stood tall and unmoving.

The women began to speak of curses and that the rain was vengeance from the gods who travelled the heavens.

Even the warriors spoke in murmurs of sorcery as they sat smoking the herb which brought them closer to the gods.

When even the priest preached of curses and magic, the people went mad and needed to look no further than Lenda for the cause of such ruin and disgrace. They surrounded the child and, seizing hold of her, marched her towards the menhir.

Stones began to rain down on the girl from all sides as she tried to shield herself with her thin white arms.

The ground began to shake as if it was sobbing: the vibrating of the menhir shook even the branches of the furthest trees.

Di U An came running, shouting in a guttural language which no one was able to comprehend.

She threw her body in front Lenda's and continued with her incomprehensible litany.

The vibrating of the menhir entered every last nerve of their bodies, causing the people to shake.

The women began to depart, followed by the warriors, who put down their stones.

Lenda was no longer just a figure of scorn and hate, she was now the object of superstition and fear, which, as the old women knew, was even worse.

Shielding the child under her cloak, she went to bargain with the priest.

The priest had never once gone against the wishes of Di U An, for he knew that to do so was to jeopardise his position, and so they were able to come to an arrangement. The child would be spared, but she was to keep within strict boundaries. She would be kept isolated from the clan and her only occupation would be to help Di U An in collecting her herbs.

Di U An was able to ensure one last compromise: anybody who touched Lenda's unholy body did so at the risk of being cursed.

It was probably this last rule which saved the child's life and ensured that she was able to grow up in peace.

Together, these taboos turned her life into a desolate wasteland of solitude.

Those Who Came Down on the Great Ship

Once, when she was eight years old, Lenda asked Di U An:

«Why am I different Di? Why am I not like the others?».

«It is the others who are different from you», Di had replied, without even looking up.

Lenda asked her no more.

Her life passed in routine and habit.

She never once considered that she was bored or that she could have something different or better than what she possessed, because she had never known any different.

In the year 10,164 Lenda was 14 years old.

The October of that year was filled with new and frightening events for the whole clan who inhabited the land of the menhir and the Di Aniut saw things they had never imagined.

For the entire month, small spherical flying craft darted rapidly through the sky.

They appeared, silently and without warning, from behind the great sun and pierced the cumulus clouds above the red mountains which stretched out the north of the land like a crown.

They would descend rapidly only to climb again at the same speed, surrounded by halos of an iridescent colour of every shade of blue and green.

The Di Aniut people were terrified at first and many refused to leave their huts, even to hunt for food.

As they spend their days keeping vigil and offering up prayers to Mut, the idea began to spread that the this was the return of those who came from the heavens and they began to view the event as a good omen.

Lenda, like everyone, knew the legends of those who came down from the heavens.

Mut was the one who reigned over the warriors and he was the God of their clan.

When she had finished her work, Lenda curled up at Di's feet and began entreating her to tell the stories of old.

And so the old woman began, always the same way, happy to be the first to pass on these memories to her.

More than any other, Lenda was fascinated by the legend of the people who walked together.

Each time, as if awakened in the memory, Di added some new detail.

«Many many years ago, when the sun was not as big as it is now and you could still see the sky, there lived a great people. This people was called the "those who walk".

«Why were they called this Di?».

«Because they were a people who were always walking, always on the move. They were hardly ever still, and travelled from one side of their land to the other without ever growing tired».

«How did they manage not to grow tired if they were always moving?».

«They had things which made them move. Things that weren't legs, or even animals. They had closed tins in which they could fit more than one at a time and tins which lifted off the ground and flew like birds. And so, they moved around in these things».

«To do what?».

The child already knew the answer, but she did not want to miss any part of Di's story.

«No one has even been able to find the answer to that question. They moved around, that was it, and as quickly as possible. But there was something else extraordinary about that people».

«What?».

«There were many of them, so many that you would not be able to count them all, and they all lived in the same place».

«All those people in one village?».

«A village so immense that you would not be able to imagine it, much bigger than all the land, so big that it stretched beyond the red mountains. And everybody lived next to one another and their roads were so full of people walking that not even a bird could have flown between them».

«Did they have warriors?».

«They had strong fearless warriors who fought battles so long and so violent that the blood flowed like rivers».

«And then Di U An? What happened next?».

«Ah, my child, what happened is that there was an immense battle and the people that walked covered their lands in the fire, a fire so great that it rose up in the sky like a great column of cloud and when it fell back down again, everything was burned».

«So the fire burned everything?».

«The fire burned warriors, women and children. It burned their villages, it burned their woods, and it turned the sky to black. All the animals and all the birds perished».

«Everything died Di».

«Everything died child».

«And Mut?».

«Mut stood by and watched. Mut only ever watches».

«Did he not care about the people who walked?».

«He cried for the birds and for the animals, he grieved for the trees».

Lenda loved to listen to the stories of those who had come down from the sky.

Since she was small, she had learned all that Di U An had known from those who came before her, about the people who, coming down from the great ships which flew like birds, had brought knowledge and wisdom to the clans.

Everything that the warriors, the women, the wise men and the midwives knew had been taught to them the men of Mut.

In reality, she had never fully understood what Mut represented, although she knew that he was the one who made the laws and governed justly those who travelled the skies.

Di had told her that on the great stone was written all that there was to know about the travellers, but none of the clan had ever had the gift to be able to understand it.

Lenda's attraction to the menhir became an obsession when, that autumn, the sky was filled with strange objects.

Every morning she made her way to the fields surrounding the menhir, making a pretence of gathering herbs, with her hood pulled down over her forehead.

She knew that in that moment she was at risk.

The people of the clan might have accused her again of being the bringer of strange events.

They might have even killed her, but this time, she was pulled by an irresistible force.

Despite endless promises to Di, every day she edged a little closer to the menhir.

«Your poor eyes will be burned out. The stele will suck you in and you won't ever return. Many have been sucked inside it Lenda, and nothing more has ever been heard of them».

But the stele seemed to call to her and draw her towards it and the young girl could not and would not resist.

She was not frightened, or even curious. It was as if she felt that contained within the monolith were the answers to her solitude and torment.

Light mists were rising off the grass, lifted by the last rays of the dying sun. She had only been there a few minutes and yet she could already feel the vibrations through her entire body.

84 She walked towards the monolith. The ground seemed as if it made of rubber, her feet lifted rhythmically as she walked, as if transported by a series of tiny waves.

She drew closer and closer.

She was right in front of the stone. It stood tall and erect, so that it appeared to pierce the sky.

She held out a hand and brushed the signs.

They were dense symbols which ran right around its sides, intertwined with figures and other designs.

She half closed her eyes as beneath her fingers the words carved into the stone began to murmur.

Lenda read word upon word, until they became stories.

The stories of millennia.

She saw figures and unnamed heroes on voyages of exploration.

She learned of the night of the times, of the great fire which had consumed the world, and she followed the wanderings of the clans down the sandy desert roads which had shut them off and saved them from the great fire.

She understood, and while the stele spoke to her, she understood who she was and felt comforted.

She belonged to that people who lived there before the clan, before all of the clans, and before the great fire.

She belonged to the people who had erected the menhir and within her she held the memories of all time.

She remained in that place, yearning for knowledge, her tiny diaphanous hands running over the figures carved in the stone.

All around her the craft darted about, coming down to touch the earth of the field, brushing against it for a moment, before disappearing behind the sun.

Far off, in the distance, Di U An watched her in silence.

The Woodpecker

Preface

A woodpecker that reminds her of her wonderful man, a bird which brings comfort as it speaks to her and which validates her every feeling, encircling her as it does like a wisp of smoke. This, in essence, is a story like no other: it is about the long and unbreakable bond which joins, beyond even life and death, two people who *truly* loved and who continue to love one another. The story is told by two people, according to their wishes, and stands as a testament to the shared love of which this couple narrates. It speaks of the true value of their bond, a bond of symbiosis and of universal goodness. Their love is an unstoppable force of nature, so much so that every hurricane, every storm of land and sea is nothing in comparison. It brings to mind a passage which I would like to share with you here:

Tell my friends that I'm dead. The water sings endlessly down where the forest is rumbling. Tell my friends that I'm dead. (The poplars are waving gauzes of sound!) Tell them I'm out here with my eyes wide open, my face covered up by this deathless bandana, the sky. Ah! Gone off without bread to my own shining star.

(FEDERICO GARCIA LORCA, from the poem *From Out Here*, transl. Jerome Rothenberg).

I am moved to believe that eternity is all-encompassing, in that that is transcends representation, being able to separate the essence of the invisible from the visible. I speak of the distorted magic of time (a concept of Mario Luzi), the sort of time which is able to stop itself and which makes no sense, which loses every reason for being, defeated by an eternity of feeling which is alive, transforming what is missing into a tangible presence.

Then there is his perfume, the smell which will not go away, which settles on the skin and in the nostrils, working its way into the crevices of the hands so that no soap on earth will wash it away.

The Woodpecker is a highly enjoyable mini novel which keeps the reader turning the page because it is not laden with unnecessary information or detail. The novel's unique structure is perhaps owing to the desire of its authors to set it down on paper, to tell their story in its immediacy, so that the future members of their family might learn by example from this testament to true love.

It will be a great example of serenity and of existential meaning. Its significance lies in the fact that it shows a right path to peace, accepting pain and strife without ever letting them assume the upper hand. What comes after will be ours if we learn to believe in it. This is where fortune lies, in *knowing*, and in being able to smile in the face of others' scepticism. But there is no place to write of that here…No, that would simply be time wasted, for some tales of fortune must be taken into our arms, held close, defended and protected.

I highly recommend this story of wisdom, which gathers together all the faiths of the world, overtaking the doubts of reason, of the notion of the brain as a physical organ, to reach the true mind, that which does not die, but which endures, giving a greater sense to what it truly means to be a human being.

SILVIA DENTI

«Do not be afraid. Fear belongs to those who do not understand».

The Woodpecker

The woodpecker was flying around and around in front of the bedroom window. Its movements were fast and graceful, punctuated by the sudden displays of acrobatics of which only woodpeckers are capable, one moment pointing its sharp beak skywards, then tucking in its coloured head and hovering for a moment, before suddenly taking flight again and plunging towards the ground.

«Do you see me?» it seemed to say.

«I see you – how could she miss it? – I see you».

There was no reason whatsoever why the woodpecker should not be able to see her. She was looking at the desk, covered in dust, and thinking that she would have to clean it. She couldn't understand how she had let it get so messy; she was normally such a tidy person. She was aware of the confusion of the last few days, of the pain, the sense of loss, of not being able to remember the small things, the things that she had always known. Then there were the other memories, those further back in time, bright and clear, like a film in Technicolor playing out before her eyes. She sat down on the perfectly made bed. Had she made it? She had no recollection of having been in bed or of having risen. It was like whole pieces of time were just erased from her memory, almost as if they had never existed. She had only been like this since *it* happened. A sudden noise shook her from her thoughts. She heard the downstairs door, the one they always used, closed with a sharp click.

«Ugo?» she said without thinking, the habit of many years spent together.

Then she remembered it couldn't possibly be him, not after what had happened. She decided to go downstairs anyway and see if anyone was there. It might have been the farmer who cut the field, or Carla who came to do the cleaning, or someone else. She couldn't remember who, but they had been so insistent. All she felt was the stress of it all, as if her brain was full of holes. That day she remembered having heard Ugo say: «Fine, you all seem to think I can't manage…but I can get by perfectly well on my own».

On his own? And her? She ran quickly downstairs and was just in time to see the figure of a man rushing out the door, slipping something into his pocket as he disappeared down the driveway. She shook her head; it wasn't possible, she knew it wasn't. Ugo was dead, dead, dead! And like all dead people he couldn't simply open and close doors or put things in his pocket. Dead. The same dull ache gnawed at her stomach as a feeling of empty desperation washed over like icy water. She couldn't remember much about that day: she saw fragments of images, of colours superimposed one over the other, heard cries, whispered words, felt hands, so many hands around her. She felt the crash and the fragments (of what?) flying around her. Then there had been the pain, but far away, detached from her, as if it belonged to another body or another person. There had been her skirt pushed up her legs, her new Indian skirt. The pain again, then blackness. My God, that darkness had swallowed her in and sucked her down into its depths. It was a dense darkness, like the water of a lake which pulled her down, only she had kicked back upwards towards the surface, or at least, she had tried to. Where had he been then? Was he already dead? Wounded? No, he wasn't there, he wasn't with her. When she had woken again she had found herself in bed, but a different bed, not her own, with people talking in breathy whispers all around her. But she wanted him. He would have held her hand and kissed behind her ears as he always did when she was afraid. He wasn't there and she was filled with the old fear of being alone. One by one, the people had left, without speaking a word of comfort to her. Only her sister had hugged her, holding her in a tight and suffocating embrace, as if she knew that she was powerless to do anything else. Alone there in the room, she had finally understood what nobody had thought to tell her: he was dead.

The next day, she didn't even remember getting up, but many people had come to visit her. It had been a strange silent sort of presence though, with no one speaking. When they turned to her with their tired eyes it was as if they were looking right through her. It was then, for the first time, that she had sensed his smell. It was unmistakable, that smell of his. She felt it all around her, invading her senses and penetrating her brain. She had not seen him, even though she had willed him to appear with every fibre of her being. She had read about apparitions and people returning when the dead person was unable to let go of their loved ones, but he had not returned, and certainly not that day. She had simply sensed him everywhere. That evening she had eaten for the first time since the accident: a bit of pasta and sauce, just as she and her Ugo liked, but she hadn't been able to finish it all. The woodpecker had appeared just as she was preparing to wash those few plates. It had begun to perform pirouettes and other acrobatic feats and as she watched it, she felt enchanted.

«Do you see me?».

«I see you».

So had begun the story of the woodpecker. From that same window she had started to see people walking down the driveway and out of the gate. Away, away, everyone away, until she was all alone. She had washed the plates and returned to the window, but the woodpecker, in its impatience, had flown away.

The Sheperd

«If you ask me, Paradise is like a huge green field, immense and infinite, without limits. It is so great that it is lost against the blue of the sky. And there are sheep everywhere, slowly grazing on the grass. Of course, what reason could they possibly have for hurrying?».

«You're right, why rush? After all, by then the worst is already over».

Now I found myself asking the same question. The shepherd repeated this idea of his over and over again until, in the end, I came to believe it myself and almost felt I could touch those sheep, with their solemn, silent gait, creatures of another dimension. Every morning at dawn it was the same story: the continuous barking of his loyal dog as it ran to round up the flock and spurn the lazier sheep on down the path which ran past the house, the hushed tinkling of the little bells around their necks, and then him, the strong rounded shoulders, the hat worn over his eyes, the grey cloak down to his feet, the boots worn in rain and shine clattering on the cobbles, the hands on his long staff, the basket of bread strapped to his body, and the flask of wine tucked into his belt. I waited for him because, with the car ready to leave, I wanted to be sure they were safely away across the fields before I left, but it was only an excuse. Truth be told, I would wait for him at first out of curiosity, but in time he came to fascinate me. I was a hospital doctor of great learning, accustomed to scientific discourse, and here I was, struck by the disarming simplicity of a man of the earth, who, for all I knew, had never opened a book in his life, the words of his day's work enough to be counted on one hand. As incredible as it was, I could not help thinking that life on earth, the life in which the whole of mankind continued to flounder, was truly strange.

At first, I used to watch from behind the curtains, afraid, careful not to intrude on the picture of that bucolic scene. As he passed by he never once lifted his head. It happened one day by chance that Susy had decided to wash the curtains, fixated as she was with keeping the house clean and tidy (an "eccentric woman" they used to call her in the village), and so I suddenly found myself exposed behind the glass, almost so that I could be seen from the outside. I only realised when it was too late. Nevertheless, that almost imperceptible sign of panic had not gone unnoticed. How it had I do not know, considering that enormous hat covered almost his entire face. By way of a reply, he stretched out his great arm in a gesture of greeting. What surprised me the most though was that he took off his hat, held it to his chest and lowered his head, almost in a bow, but without exaggeration. It was a sign of great dignity and respect, and then he was gone, without waiting for a reply.

«You were rude not to answer him», Susy scolded me.

Without being seen by the shepherd, she had witnessed the whole scene.

«It's no good looking for an excuse – she continued in the same tone – he has shown himself to be a gentleman, but not you», giving me a look which said it was pointless to try and counteract.

«Oh, no! I can't», I mumbled muttering something to myself, my pride wounded.

To wash away the stain of shame I would have to wait, even an entire day. A wait of that kind can seem either the briefest of moments or an eternity, the idea fixed in your mind as you go about your daily business.

The next day, the sun was just rising and I was already at the door. I felt a jumble of emotions, the sort which a man of my professional standing – a wizard with the scalpel, a walking encyclopaedia of science and culture – had never known of before.

«What's wrong with you this morning? You look like you've got the jitters».

Surprised and grumpy, Susy caught me as she walked into the kitchen with a huge, unstoppable yawn.

«Won't you have breakfast? What's gotten into you, Ugo? It's not like the bus passes by this way».

«I'm coming!» I replied without turning around.

I ignored the sarcastic response which I knew was coming. It didn't matter to me; I had more pressing matters at hand. I could feel inside of me that terrible childlike anxiety of the sort which never leaves us. It was like waiting for your oldest friend, wanting to be the one to greet him first, in an instant satisfying the unstoppable sense of joy growing inside you. I spent what seemed like an eternity anxiously scanning the path, then he was there and we shouted together, in unison. A shout and a cry mixed together: «Good morning, Mr Shepherd!» and, at the same time, an excited flailing of the arms.

It was childish perhaps, certainly not the height of etiquette, but it was warm and sincere. At times, it is this sort of spontaneous enthusiasm which is most captivating and surprising. A few more determined steps and he was standing before me. He was bigger than I had imagined. A mountain. I felt myself being scrutinised, right to my core. There was a moment of uncertainty and I felt like making a joke, but his gaze silenced me. He had eyes of an intense blue, and the expression of a child, astounded, shy, and yet already aware of his response: «Good morning to you, Doctor. Please, call me by my name. I am Sandro».

Hat in hand, his voice was strong and clear.

His frankness had a strange, solidifying effect, so that from then on he greeted me every morning with jokes and smiles, words to fill not a silence exactly, but a solitude which he wore lightly, for he had lived with his flock forever, or perhaps had even been born with them, and so felt himself entirely satisfied with his life.

One day, as the rain was pouring down, he confessed to me that he wanted to die with them. He politely refused the invitation to come inside.

«I would only make a mess – he turned away shyly, blushing, and then, almost as if he was confessing – and if I have any sin on my conscience, I pray to God that they will be admitted to heaven. They are without sin and of course, there are endless pastures up there. They would find a place to be sure».

«Of course – I thought, turning back inside to fetch an umbrella then hurrying to the car – there must be a heaven for all animals. What do they know of sin? They, at least, do not betray, and nor will they ever do so».

Reaching the top of the last curve, at the end of the path, he said goodbye with a wave, undeterred by the pouring rain, and as a last thought added, «Mind the mud on the road Doctor, it's dangerous».

I was in a hurry and the tarmac was slippery. I looked ahead, trying to concentrate, but I was thinking about him, about his world and its serenity, and the creatures which he loved more than children.

I was tense and on edge for all the things which were waiting for a meme and which, all of a sudden, seemed an annoyance, insignificant and stupid as they were. I was calmed by the image of the flock, slow and solemn, oblivious to the storm. One curve after another, the tyres ever more clogged with mud, all around us the red earth of mother of nature. I felt a sudden pang of anxiety, in sharp contrast with the sweet serenity of that gaze. I thought about how he pronounced the word *doctor* with startling solemnity, like a true friend, who gives everything and asks for nothing. Then there was a pothole, unexpected, hidden, followed by a great jolt, while the car continued to skid. Another corner and a last desperate attempt to regain control of the runaway vehicle. I saw the sweet imploring eyes of Susy, her arm pulling me to her, then only black, total darkness and nothing more.

The First Week

Just like that they had left and so began her first week without him. She had tried to begin with those small habits which remind us that life goes on. She woke early in the morning, with the first birdsong. Did she awake from where? With a series of mechanical movements she somehow found herself dressed, the bed perfectly made, sat in the rattan armchair. That armchair had always been the place he left his clothes. When he arrived home he threw his work suit on the armchair with a methodical gesture: jacket, tie, shirt, all bunched up and creased. Now it was empty and alone, just like her, without its usual sense of disorder.

Carla, the lady whom her family had engaged to help her, came every morning at around nine o'clock. Hearing her put the key in the lock and enter her home like it was her own felt like an invasion of her personal freedom. She forced herself to go down and greet her and instruct her on the jobs that needed doing.

«Good morning, Carla. If you could see the windows in the sitting room…».

She didn't so much as look at her, for Carla had already launched into a song with that tuneless voice of hers. She carried on talking to herself.

«Today we'll clean the sitting room windows, then the lovely lady will be happy».

Then she began to stagger up and down the step ladder with old rags of every sort.

Sometimes, someone stopped by around mid-morning. Often it was her sister-in-law, who, always in a hurry, began to give orders to Carla: «This needs doing… this needs cleaning again… this house is a disaster…» and so on, without saying anything decisive.

Her sister-in-law was completely ignored by both of them and while Carla carried on with what she was doing, she stood smiling by her side, for she knew that the whole thing would go on for another five minutes.

What had marked that first week had been the cold, or at least, the constant feeling of cold. Maybe he was cold, there where they'd put him. Even in the middle of summer he wore a jumper and always shivering under the covers in his socks. He certainly would have been cold. And she wasn't there to embrace him in her warmth, the same way you do with when a child complains of the cold. He would have felt cold and alone and there was nothing he could do about it. This made her heart tighten like a fist.

«My heart feels tight».

«It's anxiety my darling, just anxiety…no need to worry about angina…aah, my sweetheart doesn't understand anything».

They enjoyed playing doctor, and she, who truly did not understand, made sure to exaggerate everything. Then he would embrace her and say, «It's lucky I'm here, my poor little dear!».

«Oh, go run and see your *brainy* female doctor friends!».

Then they started to laugh, for he couldn't have cared less about the female doctors at work and she wasn't as stupid as she seemed. But the cold had begun to rise in her bones, so much so that she felt like she didn't have any more blood in her veins. She looked at her diaphanous hands with their translucent skin and rubbed them vigorously to try and get the blood flowing again. She put on a jumper and coat, but the room seemed even colder. She had the sensation that, in fact, the cold was not in the room, but that is emanated directly from her body. He was certainly colder though, all alone. She put up with it all, trying at all times to stand in front of the rays of the sun which burned through the half-open windows in that sad month of July.

Sometimes the woodpecker came to keep her company, setting down on the windowsill and turning its little head with its long red beak.

«Do you see me? I see you».

«I can see you too», then in a flash it was gone, flown back to who knows what nest.

Everything that had been before was gone and he wasn't there. The cold which gnawed at her bones became a part of life and at times it was almost as if she couldn't feel it. One day, early in the morning, she decided to put their photographs in order. She had always loved those ambiguous icons, in which what appeared could or could not be real. She found in them the reflection of life, especially those which bore a date and were in black and white, where the figures stood frozen and fixed in time. The first photo she found was of him as a boy, shovelling snow outside his beloved family home in Bologna. His grandfather had been a senator and the house had been in his family for many generations. Their nobility meant that they were not the sort of people to be troubled by the everyday events which shape the lives of others. He denied it, but he still had something of the nobleman in him, the sort of person who did not understand the value of money or the need to rake the autumn leaves.

Nevertheless, he had been ready to learn from her, a country girl to the core, and perhaps, in his "noblesse" he admired her ability to always make things work without much to-do. He had been so handsome back then, harbouring a sort of veiled sexuality which she had continued to see in him even when his hair turned grey and age began to catch up with him. Then there was him at the Navy Academy, smiling, even if she knew that it was only on the outside that he seemed happy. He was an artistic soul, but the rigours and discipline of academy life took away his will to fly.

His desire to fly was what had first united them from the very beginning: no net, no cage, no limits. Truth be told, she had been jealous at times, of him, of his women, all loved, because that's the way he was. Really, however, it was that she was jealous of his role, for their unique bond was untouchable by any man or woman. Photos and then more photos, all of the two of them.

It was then, as she was looking at the photo of the two of them in Bologna, the one where he was kissing her neck, that she felt (or did she see?) him for the first time since the accident. The cold turned into the sensation of an all-encompassing embrace: the warm hands and the annoyance she felt when he embraced her with both arms and legs when they were in bed, so that she was unable to move. She felt his intense smell all around her.

The House Of Fichino

The first time that Susy saw "Fichino", just a stone's throw from Casciana Terme, beneath the mountains to the north of Pisa, she was immediately drawn to the enormous red and white colonial mansion, now somewhat rundown following the death of my parents.

«So this is going to be our home», she exclaimed, turning a sudden pirouette in the high grass of the garden, like a little girl excited by an unexpected treasure.

This was followed by a pause, as she looked around to make sure it wasn't all just a dream, like Alice in Wonderland, happy and serene after so trials and tribulations. The Irish girl in her continued to dance barefoot on the crest of that windswept hill, her red hair flowing about her shoulders. Then she fell breathless into my arms, her cheeks flushed, as if she had just run «a joyful race to the top of the hill», as a poet might have written. «Soft, warm and sensual» I would have added, though I am certainly no poet.

«I feel – she whispered as she kissed me – In Ireland we say this when we feel something profound, a unique sensation which grows inside you, shakes you to your core and makes your heart beat faster».

Then she held me in a tight embrace, penetrating and infinite, which contained her every desire to live and to hope.

«Do you see Ulisse?» pointing out the great white dog which raced breathlessly back and forth, disappearing and reappearing amongst the grass.

«He too is free again. I felt inside myself that this was how it would be. The other day, when I went to the kennels I didn't see him at first, but he saw me. He called out to me and I answered him. Now we are truly free, all of us together».

That's right, Ulisse. This was the other side of Susy, the lesser-known side of her character, but just as real as the rest of her. She adored animals more than humans, with the exception of ants and insects, which were her sworn enemies. So, in short, with Ulisse and the others, that made six dogs and two dwarf rabbits. The Tibetan goat and horses had gradually left us, the first for reasons of safety, the second for cost and the difficulty of taking care of them. And so, between us there had sprung up an earthly paradise, while we two, like a newly created Adam and Eve, spent our days as country people, not farmers exactly, but in a happy, healthy life full of dreams.

Yes, perhaps I'm living in a dream world when I say this, for like Adam and Eve, we too were humiliated by those who loved us, expelled from the world which gave birth to us, so that we felt broken but not deterred. The glue which bound us was our love, greater than what came about after a fortuitous encounter some time before in an anonymous school room, and much stronger than those who tried to divide us expected. From all to nothing, from nothing to all.

If you think about it, heaven and earth are not so far apart. All you need to do is believe. Because many of the things you find here you also find up there. A friend interested in the paranormal had told me this once and truth be told, I had no reason to doubt him, especially in the light of testimonials from those who sought contact with their dead relatives.

«Animals, for example, are good – specified my friend – and therefore, there is no doubt that they go to heaven».

Many speak of a happy place, where man and beast live together in peace, while others say that to reach it you simply need to concentrate your thoughts on it before falling asleep, which is a sort of sweet death. Once you find yourself there it is difficult to choose the path back again. Waking up always leaves behind a bitter taste, for the soul cannot hide its desire to return to that place.

Susy and I often spoke of it while seated on the porch, the cool summer breeze blowing down from the hill as it did every evening to take the edge off the suffocating heat of the day. These moments were important for us, moments which took away the sense of anxiety and fear of the world, giving us the will to not give in, to keep moving ahead, without looking back. One particularly dramatic day it actually happened and we didn't go there again. Today, we don't feel any sense of loss. All the family we need is right here.

Shadows

His smell remained as a powerful presence in the room. Carla came in the morning, entering as if she was the mistress of the house, opening all the windows and passing her dusters over the furniture. The smell of detergent invaded the bedroom, but nothing could take away his scent. It was that scent, his alone, which, many years before, had allowed her to recognise him amongst many others.

Only God knows if she had had to struggle to make him notice her. He did not see or sense the world in the same way that she did; for like an animal, she categorised people according to their scent. But she had immediately sensed that he would have been capable of it, to "smell", he who based everything on the ability to "understand". The possibility was there and the prognosis, as he would have said, was good. She had really tried. She saw the shadow all of a sudden, before she heard the door open and close straight after. The smell was stronger and his warmth enveloped her. But she couldn't see him. There was a sort of trembling transparent form over behind the door to their room. But was it possible to see through doors?

She didn't question it further. What was that line from *Hamlet*? «There are more things in heaven and earth, Horatio, than are dreamt of in your philosophy».

It was a truism like many others written by the English poet. To be able to see beyond that door was, perhaps, one of them. She was disappointed, however, that he did not come into the room. She wanted him to see her, to kiss her, to greet her with that ironic and unique gaze of his. It was as if he had run from something he did not want to see. Door opened, closed, and away. The woodpecker landed on the windowsill. It sat very still, with its tail trembling, which was unusual. «Do you see me? I see you».

«I see you too».

But it was him she wanted to see. The woodpecker looked at her with its penetrating black eyes, but it was a look of disbelief, as if she didn't understand and it was unable to explain.

«Why haven't you left this house? Why, after what happened, have you decided to stay?».

«I have nowhere else to go. I belong to this house, like him».

«You must accept what has happened. It would have been easier for everyone if you hadn't decided to stay. Can't you see that?».

She decided that the woodpecker was stupid. After all, if there were creatures resembling humans which were stupid, then a woodpecker could be one of them.

«He has stayed too», she replied like a stupid little girl.

The woodpecker obviously agreed with her because it flew away without so much as a reply.

But she was as stubborn as a mule and she had already decided that not only did she have to see the shadow again, but she also had to break through that delicate veil and have her man back again, feel his hands, his body. If he had decided to stay there must be a reason and she would have had him back body and soul if it was the last thing she did.

She walked over to the window and closed it, for the cold had returned. In *her* garden Carla was watering the flowers.

All of a sudden, as she was moving away from the window and was already behind the curtains, Carla let out a cry, but a piercing cry, a cry of pure terror.

Ulisse

The cry did not concern her, but she felt obliged to go down and see what had happened. Perhaps Carla had seen a mouse or a grass snake, which looks so frightening, but in the end are harmless.

Out in the park Carla had the watering pump in her hand, but she stood there without the usual sing-song voice and her eyes fixed on nothing. There was no doubt it, she had seen a snake, for only a snake could make her stop singing. What concerned her instead was Ulisse, her dog, the last of her brood. He was standing there in the middle of the lawn, still as a lizard, with his tongue out and tail wagging as he did when he was excited. Knowing that Carla did not have that effect on him, she was worried.

«Uli, my love, what is it?».

The dog's tail was turning like a blender and the woodpecker, which had suddenly returned, nonplussed by the great creature: «He sees you».

This was good news: she was certain that Ulisse could see her. She walked up to the dog to scratch its head, something which he loved, but he whimpered. His tail still wagging, he ran over to his place under the pine tree in front of the gate, from where he liked to watch out for everyone and everything. He continued to look at her though and so she waved to him as she always did.

The sky had filled with clouds which threatened rain, the sort which appears in the country and near the hills and she, in her thin jumper, feeling the usual cold, decided to go back inside.

Out of habit, she looked first to see that the dogs were sheltered. She saw them all in their kennels, with their muzzles pointed towards her inquiringly, a sad look on their faces. Then came his voice (unmistakable): «Everyone inside, it's about to rain».

Ulisse didn't move, but that was not unusual for him. Ulisse was a strange dog, exceptional in many ways. He had given him to her, understanding the emptiness in her life.

They had been living in Bologna at the time. Bologna, the place she loved more than any other. The place where she was truly happy. But in the same moment that she realised how much she loved it she knew that she would lose it, because she always lost the things she truly loved. It was as if life was always telling her to make the best of it.

To cut a long story short, one torrid afternoon, the sort where in Bologna you're barely able to take a step, they had decided to go and fetch the unfortunate creature in the most wretched place possible for a dog, the kennels. They had chosen the worse place possible on such a hot and muggy day, Marzabotto. Finding the kennels was one of the most difficult things they had ever done in their lives, and this despite the fact that they had been all over the world, including the deserts of North Africa, which were nothing in comparison. Even Livingstone, the great explorer, would have lost his way. Together, however, they were a team and they managed to find it. Of all the possible kennels it was the least scrupulous and the worker who greeted them conducted them with the arrogance of a sister on a hospital ward. Ugo, still afflicted by a thirst for learning, listened to her like the Oracle at Delphi or some great university professor, which, if you think about it, are the same thing. She, on the other hand, wanted to let her senses guide her and wasn't listening at all. And she was right to do so, for it was then that she smelled him.

He called her inside, inside his soul, pulling her in with those black eyes in which the whole of mankind could have drowned.

The ward sister wasn't convinced: «Difficult dog, madam, not adoptable. He's been mistreated and is untrainable. He's capable of attacking and can give a nasty bite».

She looked at Ugo as she said this, his undeniable charm clearly has affected her as well.

As it was, this difficult dog permitted a collar to be put on it like a pedigree poodle and allowed itself to be carried off by her out of love and with a love for which it would have given its life. From that day forth they had felt a deep connection, so deep that they saw into the other's soul. She and Ugo had bought and adopted other dogs over the years, but though they loved them all, for her and for the both of them, Ulisse was the most special.

And so that day too, Ulisse consoled her by staying fixed to his spot under the pine tree, like always. «See, I'm still here, watching over you».

In the strangeness of the days that followed, seeing him there was a great comfort to her.

The Bear

With surprising agility, the bear moved amongst the river rapids. Its great paws seemed like hands as it attempted to grab hold of the salmon which swam upstream to deposit their eggs. Amazingly, it was successful. Oh, how successful!

She was watching a documentary in that humid summer's afternoon. Her bare feet on the tiles, her shirt open at the collar she did not feel the heat which caused Carla to grumble without rest.

To tell the truth, she felt a cold shiver run down her neck from time to time, but she loved the feeling of her bare feet on the floor so much that she refused to put her shoes back on.

The cold did not frighten her. She had not felt the cold this much since she and Ugo had decided to come and live in that magical, out-of-the-way house, amongst orchards of fig trees, with the four winds battering it in summer and winter. She felt the wind most of all in the winter when it cut the mouth like a knife and paralysed the fingers, even with gloves on. The winter before the accident, she had been waiting for Ugo in the room with the fireplace, with the fire lit and the flames roaring, carefully tended by her.

She liked him to come home to a roaring log fire, even if perhaps he did not realise the effort she went to and who, with droughts and the like, understood nothing of it and had to make do with firelighters and newspaper, or dried olive branches. He would then come home and say «What a lovely hot fire Susy», as if to light it had been the easiest thing in the world.

It was in those moments, incredibly, that she loved him more than ever because he had the same sense of enchantment as a child. But those days were now over and that winter, perhaps, she might not have lit the fire. A modern halogen heater would have been enough for the cold inside that house which would not go away. That was not entirely true: the cold turned to the sweetest warmth whenever she saw the shadow. The shadow had, by now, become a constant of her day.

She was no longer afraid as she had been at the beginning, but awaited the flickering of its non-colours, of its rapid movements, and the light which sometimes preceded it.

She did not have the courage to ask anyone about, in part also because no one spoke to her directly. She believed that Carla could see her though, because every now and then she let out a sudden scream which made the hairs on her arms stand on end and the dogs howl. Stupid woman! To frighten the children like this, as Ugo used to call them.

She was good, however, and obeyed her orders, even if, in reality, she had not given her any. Once, in a half sleep which felt more like torpor, she had seemed to hear his voice far away speaking with Carla.

«You need to lift up the seats to clean under the table properly, Carla. You know how much my wife would have complained… – and inside herself, not thinking, she had said – Complain? Do I really?».

But then she was woken from the torpor and the dream had remained with all the others. The shadow, however, was seen more and more frequently until, day after day, as the event was repeated, she came to realise something: the outline was becoming ever clearer, the subtle nuances of nothingness, in that movement of forms, the shadow began to take on a greater clarity which came to assume characteristics and features.

It was then that she had the feeling that someday soon she would be able to perceive the face of the shadow. Instead of frightening her she saw it as something good. After all, was she not a shadow herself?

Memories

She sometimes found herself remembering how they had been before. Her memories were not thoughts, but still images which appeared in rapid succession like photographs. The sensation she had had since the beginning was that the two of them were born with their love for one another and that the past did not exist for either of them. As it was, their past did exist and it was as heavy and cumbersome as a boulder. It was the sort of past which leaves you with scars, which are ever more painful with every season that passes. So similar were their respective stories that it was incredible, stories which spoke of disaster, whose protagonists were intelligent, sensitive people, while the aggressive, unstable individuals were bit-part characters or "guest stars".

The first time she saw him was at the hospital ward. At the time Ugo was, in her own words, a neurosurgeon by chance, or, as she came to understand, a footballer and writer with a surgeon's scalpel in his hands. He was conscientious and kind as only those who have a true calling for medicine are.

As it was, she didn't care at all what he did. He could have been anything: she fell in love with him because of who he was inside. There had been no falling in love, it was simply love at first sight. Her heart told her that though there were richer, more handsome, more intelligent men out there, for her there was only him.

And so it was. They did not see one another again for years. Perhaps, though it was part of the mechanisms of destiny, for a love like theirs could not be measured by normal standards. Then one day they met by chance and never left each other again. The choice was made unconsciously, over and above everyone and everything else, and she never regretted it for a minute.

When they bickered, for example, he would say in a proud, provocative tone: «Go, if you want to go, just do it. If this is not what you want then just go!».

Secretly, though, she thought he was stupid, because there was nowhere for either of them to go if not together. There was no other place for them but that house, the walls of which spoke of the stories and emotions seen there. It was not simply a house they lived in, but a container of souls and of memories.

As they speak of in fairy tales, they had remained there ever after. He had stayed behind after the accident, she was sure of it now. The shadow was his soul, unable to leave that place. But where then? Maybe there was nowhere else for him to go but the house. The shadow now belonged to her daily life. It moved through the rooms and seemed to follow her, or was she the one following the shadow?

He said at the kitchen table, in that great room, sometimes his head between his hands. He seemed desperate in those moments, and so she sat in front of him and stroked his head. «Can you see me? I'm here with you».

But he didn't move, not even to lift his head. Only the woodpecker seemed to see her, and in those dark moments, it would tap on the blinds with gusto. He too heard the destructive bird and saw it. At the sound of its hammering on the wood he lifted his head and smiled. Then he hung his head again, as if he had neither the will nor the strength to shoo it away.

Emerging From The Coma

To die to sleep, to sleep, perchance to dream. I don't want to brag on about Shakespeare, for the love of God, but for a simple shrink and neurosurgeon like myself, the divide between this world and the next is, no more and no less, the clinical state of coma, something which is better even than sleep and dreams.

Despite my many years of medical practice, I still sometimes manage to laugh when someone talks of coming out of an irreversible coma. While I understand the tragedy and sense of hope, either you believe in miracles and everything falls into place, or the diagnosis is simply wrong. In short, or you don't come back and no one will ever know the truth about what awaits us after death, or you do and then there spring up a thousand stories about the experience, some more reliable than the others.

In any case, it is life, in all its humdrum monotony that you lose, nothing more. It's no good getting worked up about it; you're never going to get it back. And even if a whole year went by, you would never remember your real age. Ah, the tricks of destiny. In any case, with the gift of hindsight, there are a thousand memories to dazzle and amaze you, although they last only a second. And what you perceive are muffled and faraway voices, the person you are watching is only an expressionless statue, because the person who is really alive is you, even if no one, in the whole of that agonising wait, knows it.

«I saw the angels – I remember – and whether you believe in them or not I felt like I was one of them. There was a great light all around. And then faces, so many faces and hands, many many hands, all united, together. It was beautiful, so beautiful. Why then would I want to come back».

Now I say: «Susy, come back to me, I'm waiting for you».

Maria

In her solitude she did at least have one friend. Ugo's mother Maria came to visit her at the same time every day. In the early morning, when the dreaming moon makes way for the overbearing sun, they would meet at the vine-covered gazebo.

Maria waited for her on the stone bench and as soon as she saw her emerge onto the porch she gave her a little wave with her hand. She had thought that Maria had died years before, following a terrible illness. She had believed it because she had lived that moment. She hadn't seen Maria. No, she had "felt" her die one June night. All of nature had come to a standstill, including the stars, and a great wind had come into her room, blowing the curtains and opening the closed windows. It was in this way that her love had taken itself away with her by the hand. And then Maria, or her body, had seemed like a happy girl who has just seen her young love.

Maria, dead? She didn't ask herself any more about it, as she rarely did these days. She was not the Maria she remembered, the one struck down by illness and riddled with open sores. She was a well turned-out old lady, her hair and clothes always immaculate just like the other women of her generation.

He intelligent, inquiring eyes always looked at her when she spoke of her troubles and doubts. She spoke little, but her smile was like a balm which soothed all the pain and worries of recent weeks.

«Ugo is like this – she said, consoling her – he can't help himself. But he will have to decide whether or not he can rise above this, forget and start again on his own. He's a good boy, as you know, but he's also the most fragile and sensitive of my children».

«Mamma, why has Ugo come back? Can you really come back?».

«You know that you can».

She did not know at all, but she sat there and continued to listen to her. Sometimes Maria would speak of her old stories, of her dreams. She spoke little of the love for her husband out of modesty. As she told her stories the time flew by.

«Susanna, it's not Ugo who has come back!».

What exactly did she mean?

The woodpecker returned with the rising of the sun over the hills and hopped around them with its usual exuberance. When Maria prepared to leave (she never asked where she went), the woodpecker followed her, matching its flight with the steps of the old lady.

It was one morning, just after she had left their usual appointment that she understood. Maria, that morning, as she was preparing to leave, had caressed her hand.

«Do not be afraid. Fear belongs to those who do not understand».

She had then walked back towards the house and gone into the kitchen. Ugo was having breakfast. His shadow was, by now, properly defined and she was able to see him clearly, with his ruffled hair which told her that he'd just got out of bed.

He was sat at the table with a glass of milk preparing a sandwich. He hadn't put down any plate and the jam was certain to mix with the crumbs on the table. He would never have done that if she had been there.

She went up to him and looked at him. She stared him right in the eyes, but they looked right through her, indifferent. «Ugo, there are crumbs on the table!».

He did not so much as blink. He would never have behaved that way if she had been there. It was then that she understood. It was him who wasn't there. She was the one left behind. It was in that moment that the pain consumed her whole being as the cold continued to eat away at her soul.

The woodpecker knocked on the shutters.

«I see you».

It turned back and flew away into the garden.

At Home After The Storm

It is true that my colleagues in Accident and Emergency already thought I was a goner. It was laughable to think there was anything more to say about the coma. I was dead to the world. Period. But as Susy used to say, if you're time isn't up, you can still pull through. And that was what happened.

And yet, if to die and leave your loved ones behind, and be aware of it is torture enough, no less desperate is emerging from the dark to discover that in your place was the person who had smiled at you that day, a moment before the accident. To speak of life and light when your light, that which lit up you every waking moment, is now extinguished, truly is the worst kind of emptiness.

It is a hundred times better to die, no contest. To be able to hear her through the silence but not see her was an unbearable solitude, an agony without end. Even that woodpecker which I can see now as it flies around the garden and which, perhaps, I had never noticed before that moment, seems to look at me in a certain way, as if it knows the cause of my suffering. Or maybe it really is her, come back in that form. Think what you like, but some mysterious and aching force tells me I'm right. She truly is a strange and extraordinary being, my Susy.

Un libro dona libertà, conoscenza, è la possibilità di vivere esperienze nuove e diverse. Spesso però il maggiore ostacolo alla lettura di un nuovo libro è il prezzo. Non solo, talvolta l'opera è irreperibile, oppure (è il caso di alcuni ebook) di difficile lettura, incompatibile con i diversi ebook-reader.

Se il libro ha già un secolo d'età, probabilmente è scritto in un linguaggio desueto, talvolta i riferimenti e le note non sono in grado di dialogare con il lettore.

FdBooks offre i grandi testi del passato sia in cartaceo che in digitale, a un ottimo prezzo, in italiano e in lingua inglese.

Ogni edizione cartacea è pubblicata a un prezzo bassissimo, ogni edizione digitale è curata nell'impaginazione e fornita di ulteriori contributi. Quando possibile, per i soli libri in lingua italiana, sono aggiunte note e corretti i refusi per una maggiore attualizzazione e comprensione da parte del lettore.

Si tratta di **un impegno editoriale che esige grande caparbietà e passione**. I libri in catalogo sono tutti esenti da diritti di pubblicazione, ovvero gli autori sono di norma deceduti almeno settant'anni fa. Dunque **ogni opera in catalogo è pubblica**, è già di tutti. **FdBooks** ne cura l'edizione con una corretta impaginazione, corregge i refusi, aggiunge note se necessario e redige le due versioni cartacea e digitale. A un prezzo molto basso per il lettore.

L'auspicio è che un giorno una vasta comunità sarà in grado di condividere beni e servizi a un prezzo sociale, ovvero scambiandoli con altri beni e servizi se necessario. Un sistema economico alternativo a quello odierno, che non scalzerà il modello capitalistico attuale, ma si accosterà a esso.

Apparendo così in **tutta la sua bellezza**.

FdB

ABW

Author's Best Works

In the series *Author's Best Works*, FdBooks offers a selection of the best authors in world literature. Each book has interactive footnotes and chapter headings in clear and elegant typeset, and is available at a very affordable price. Because… *Culture is priceless, almost always*

Auto da fé

Una collana di nuove opere (esordienti e non) per consentire a tutti di pubblicare *gratis* il proprio manoscritto. La collana ha per nome *Auto da fé*, poiché l'atto di fede più importante è quello dell'autore nei confronti di se stesso, prima di rimettersi al pubblico giudizio.

Printed by CreateSpace, An Amazon.com Company

Available from Amazon.com, CreateSpace.com, and other retail outlets

9 781973 991144